Editorial

This editorial may be the last one I write in my editorial office in Cross Street. *PN Review* has been published from here since November 2002 (*PNR* 148).

Its first permanent address was at the Corn Exchange, Manchester, for twenty-five years, until we were evicted by an IRA bomb in 1996. We spent a brief exile in Salford but settled into salubrious offices in Cross Street, along from St Anne's Church where Thomas de Quincey was baptised, and where a homeless man asleep on a bench turns out to be a bronze Jesus displaying the stigmata. We are cater-corner from William Gaskell's Unitarian Chapel where the publisher Charles Dickens occasionally attended services with his author Elizabeth (she contributed to *Household Words* where he was the 'conductor'). When *PN Review* and Carcanet first settled, the chapel still stood; it has since been ingested (still a chapel) into a large office building. L.S. Lowry frequented the chop house in Chapel Walk and survives as a corpulent bronze at the bar. We arrived here on 27 November 2002.

PNR 149 was assembled, the Editorial and News & Notes written, at this cluttered readers' table, a gift from the Central Library after the bomb. A patient schoolboy has pressed into the tooled leather covering with a blunt pencil, 'Hession is Gay'.

Thumbing through *PNR 149*, I expected I would enter a different world. Twenty-two years is a generation in poetry. But no. My editorial squared up against the American government:

> Christopher Ross of the American State Department coordinates 'public diplomacy'. He is keen to revive government sponsored cultural programmes abroad. Speaking the increasingly familiar language of cultural economics, he declares that such activities are a 'cost-effective investment to ensure US national security', a means of countering 'the skewed, negative and unrepresentative' image of America that, in his view, mass communications convey. Writers are suddenly in the front line when it comes to national security, not cannon fodder but the cannons themselves.

The first and second topics in News and Notes had contemporary resonance. The second reported how Irish-resident French novelist Michel Houellebecq 'was acquitted by a Paris court of charges of inciting racial hatred when he declared in an interview last year that Islam was "the most stupid religion".' Three Muslim associations and the Human Rights League in Paris brought the case.

The first item was more immediate.

> Tom Paulin, invited to lecture at Harvard, had his invitation revoked when a number of people – academics, students and alumni – took umbrage at comments he made to an Egyptian newspaper in April. Brooklyn born Jews who had settled in the West Bank, he said, 'should be shot dead,' adding, 'I think they are Nazis, racists; I feel nothing but hatred for them.'

Pressure of an old-fashioned, increasingly unfamiliar sort was exerted and 'the invitation to lecture at Harvard was restored after a flurry of publicity, in the interests of "free speech".' Paulin issued an apology, unsaying what he had in fact said. The late Professor Helen Vendler put the record straight:

> On the basic principle of freedom of speech, Harvard University was right to reinstate its invitation to the poet Tom Paulin. It should be noted, however, that Mr Paulin is himself committed to the censorship of political opinions with which he does not agree. Last year Mr Paulin wrote to *The Guardian*, in London, asking why it permitted 'Zionists' like me and the author and critic Ian Buruma to write for and express our views in the paper. He is also a supporter of the boycott of Israeli academics, denying those who (like me) deplore the policies of the current Israeli government the right to speak in international forums, solely on the basis of their nationality.

Plus ça change. But, no: there are radical changes to acknowledge. News & Notes in this issue, twenty-two years on, is quiet. The burning issues of the new century appear to have been displaced by a sad necropolis. An abundance of death notices. Poets do grow old and prove their mortality, but so many...

Contemporary issues affecting writers are as numerous and challenging as they were in 2002. But they are toxic and divisive in a different way. *PNR* has grown circumspect, cautioned by its public patrons, at times cajoled by its allies. Indirection becomes the indicated route.

Not a comfortable route. The universal mantras of inclusion can feel, can *be* hostile to an insistence on editorial selectivity and the judgement of relative value implicit in making choices. The request that performance poetry exist also as compelling and coherent text might find itself dismissed as elitist. Specialists and learned readers are stigmatised for their knowledge, however generous they are in sharing it. In a radio interview not long ago I was asked for an 'expert opinion' on a piece of popular verse: then the presenter said, 'We've heard what the Professor has to say – what do *you* think?' to my eager fellow contributor. The word 'Professor' carried at least six sibilants, like the serpent in the garden. It can feel like a time of devaluation, dismantling, demolition, a privileging of 'the other' even when its otherness is not understood. A time of forked tongues, not always the serpent's.

Amazing how much mud sticks to one's boots after twenty-two years. Leaving the Corn Exchange was much easier, barefoot.

Letters to the Editor

Mark Dow writes: Some readers might be interested in this footnote on prosody.

In our 2021 interview (*PNR* 263), Nigel Fabb and I briefly discussed T.S. Omond's *A Study of Metre* (1903) and its attempt to replace scansion by syllables with scansion by 'time-spaces'. I asked Fabb if Omond's book is much discussed by linguists, and he replied, 'I cannot think of anyone referring to it.'

I have since come across a discussion of Omond by Catherine Ing in her *Elizabethan Lyrics: A Study of the Development of English Metres and their Relation to Poetic Effect* (1951). Ing explains that Omond's 'isochronous periods' are what we typically call feet, and she writes: 'I believe that Omond's 'syllabic variety with temporal uniformity' is a true and illuminating suggestion if we interpret it elastically: if we substitute for 'uniformity' some word like 'balance' or 'proportion'; and if we look for this balance or proportion in units larger than that of the foot.'

Mark Haworth-Booth writes: I was very interested by the letter from Dave Wynne-Jones on 'Political Content, and Discontent' in issue 277. He noted that 'even though some Palestinian poets are being featured online, where else is the political poetry about the catastrophe in Gaza?' He added that 'Within my workshop group, poets seem to be struggling with the enormity of what is happening, but the performance poetry circuit could have been expected to have more nimbleness and resilience in its responses. Unfortunately, there seems to have been a marked lack of engagement there too.'

I am chair of the North Devon branch of the Palestinian Solidarity Campaign. We have held Gaza vigils in Barnstaple High Street since October. Each week several people will read out texts – which are often poems and often by Palestinian writers. The poem 'If I must die' by Refaat Alareer (assassinated by the Israeli military on 6 December) has been read on many occasions. Kites have been made, inscribed with words from the poem, and brought to our vigils. We have heard poems by Abdelfattah Abusrour, Mahmoud Darwish, Suheir Hammad, Aurora Levins Morales, Michael Rosen, Lena Khalaf Tuffaha and many others. I wonder how widely this has been replicated around the country. I have never known so much poetry to be recited in our streets and listened to so intently by gatherings ranging from twenty to forty people. Local poets have read their own efforts too, often written in response to the latest news. Since October, I have found it difficult to write about anything other than Gaza.

Years ago an article in the *TLS* referred to the 'crowd poets' of ancient Greece. I've always thought Adrian Mitchell was a fine modern example of this, especially when I heard him belt out 'To Whom It May Concern' ('Tell me lies about Viet Nam'). Perhaps some of mine are 'crowd' or street poems, especially the one involving call-and-response with those present. I've read others to poetry groups away from the streets and been touched by the applause that followed each Gaza poem: people seem to need to hear Gaza poems and to acknowledge them.

News and Notes

I'll put you through to Biography • *John McAuliffe writes:* The Irish poet Gerald Dawe has died in Dublin, after a long illness. He was seventy-two. Known to all as Gerry, he grew up in Belfast and attended the same school as his friend Van Morrison, then studying at the University of Ulster and at UCG, now the University of Galway, where he taught for a number of years. He moved to Dublin in 1992, taught at Trinity College, and co-founded and subsequently directed that University's creative writing MA at The Oscar Wilde Centre.

Gerry is remembered by many as a great teacher. Enthusiasms and advocacy also marked his writing life. He founded and co-edited for many years the Irish literary journal *Krino*, and also edited or introduced selections from poets as varied as Charlie Donnelly, Padraic Fiacc, Ethna McCarthy and Gerald Fanning, as well as the outstanding *Earth Voices Whispering: An Anthology of Irish War Poetry 1914–1945*. His *Cambridge Companion to Irish Poets* (with Cambridge UP) was excoriated for its lack of women contributors and subjects, something Dawe sought to rectify by his support for Poetry Ireland's 2018 day conference *Missing Voices: Irish Women Poets of the 18th-20th Century*. A later poem, 'The Lost', is less sanguine about the effects of the associated social media campaigning: 'After the denunciation they came piling in...'.

Alongside his teaching and editorial work, he published nine books of poetry with The Gallery Press. His last book, whose title nods to Auden, *Another Time: Poems 1978–2023*, has just been announced as the winner of the annual O'Shaughnessy Prize for Poetry. Reticent, wry and acute, Dawe's poems are often miniatures, occasionally stretching to sequences. They include recoveries of his Belfast childhood, or the kinds of encounter or shaded places which might have appealed to the Gaston Bachelard of *Intuitions of the Instant* or *The Poetics of Space*. A typically resonant poem from the 'Resolution and Independence' sequence runs in its entirety: 'Qualm at Waterstone's / *Hold on*, she said, / *I'll put you through to Biography / and they'll look for you there*.'

Vincent O'Sullivan, KNZM, 8 September 1937–28 April 2024 • *Kirsty Gunn writes:* The world turns, and in New Zealand it was already the next day when we heard news of the death of the New Zealand poet Vincent O'Sullivan. Immediately tributes started pouring in from across the international community of Katherine Mansfield scholars and writers which he had seemed, singlehandedly, to have established. His founding work on the short story writer – his scholarship and writing and the many editions of her fiction and nonfiction which he either compiled himself or inspired others to put together, including the vast project of *The Collected Letters* for Oxford University Press – established Mansfield as a serious modernist who had more than earned her place among Eliot, Woolf, Joyce and the rest. All of it has been achieved in a prose that is infused with his own poetic understanding and sense.

Altogether there were twenty collections of O'Sullivan's verse – the last of which, 'As Is', is published this June by Te Herenga Waka University Press. He was Poet Laureate of New Zealand from 2013–15 and knighted for services to literature in 2021. I saw him towards the end of March at his home in Port Chalmers, the veranda outside the window of the light-filled sitting room in which we spoke a tumble of late white roses. It felt like summer, but in New Zealand it would be winter soon. He was funny and gracious and full of news of universities both here and there; Oxford and Otago and Edinburgh and Victoria University as it once was... These places were all walked through, doors opened and closed within them, gardens and common rooms traversed, conversations and debates and conversations listened into and appreciated – or abhorred. He was aghast, as are so many in New Zealand, to learn that Victoria University was to lose its chair in Shakespeare studies. 'It takes only one generation not to be taught Shakespeare for the next never to have heard of him', Vincent said. So yes, he was thinking about that sort of thing, along with the final edits on the new collection as well as wanting news of poetry in Scotland. I had a pile of recent publications for him to go through, and we talked of them, and of ballads and of Burns Singer, and of the last poem for his new collection that he'd just finished. Not one of his beautifully modulated sentences, funny and thoughtful and self-deprecating and erudite, and all at once, was wasted on the subject of his own mortality – yet mortality rested there, as he spoke, quietly breathing. It was the same sound that we hear in so much of his work, poetry and prose. As the poet and translator Michael Hulse has written, 'Vincent's voice is in my head'.

Different universes • *Kate Farrell writes:* The poet David Shapiro died on 4 May at the age of seventy-seven. Shapiro grew up in Deal, NJ, a violin prodigy in an artistic family. Deciding at ten to be a poet, he made a plan to read every book of poetry in the Newark Public Library. He kept falling in love, he reported, with new poets without giving up the earlier ones: 'a different poet would be a different universe'. The start, perhaps, of the open-armed, wide-minded pluralism that would buoy and energize his thought and writing. Shapiro himself was something of a walking, talking library; his conversation, a 'tapestry of quotes', the poet-critic Don Share wrote, 'profound and resounding... quirky and endlessly edifying'.

At fifteen, Shapiro met Kenneth Koch, Frank O'Hara, John Ashbery and the movement now known as the New York School – of which he would become in time a leading poet, exponent and scribe. He studied with Koch at Columbia University, as a freshman publishing *January*, the first of eleven books of poetry. After earning his MA at Clare College, Cambridge, he returned to Columbia for a PhD.

His *New York Times* obituary quotes the poet Ron Padgett: 'David Shapiro wrote poems that sound like no one else's, poems full of mystery, lyricism, and agile leaps of an eternally fresh spirit, with surprising humour in his unearthly melancholy.' Shapiro also produced works of prose, including monographs on Ashbery, Jasper Johns and Piet Mondrian. He taught literature, art history, cinema and cross-disciplinary courses at Columbia, William Paterson University, and the Irwin S. Chanin School of Architecture at the Cooper Union. A new book by Shapiro – *You Are the You: Writings and Interviews on Poetry, Art, and the New York School* – edited by me, with a foreword by David Lehman, is due out from MadHat Press.

Singing high and low • *Sunil Iyengar writes*: The American poet Joseph Harrison died last February at the age of sixty-six. He was celebrated at a Baltimore memorial service in June. Participants included some of the city's best-known poets – most of whom are associated with the John Hopkins University Writing Seminars: Mary Jo Salter, David Yezzi, Dora Malech and Greg Williamson.

In his own poems, Harrison's use of elaborate verse patterns, rhyme and metre, and literary allusions, far from appearing schematic or contrived, could yield startling discoveries. His virtuosic range was matched by the breadth of his admirers, who included Harold Bloom, John Ashbery, Richard Wilbur, and particularly Anthony Hecht. Introducing Harrison's debut collection, *Someone Else's Name* (2003), Hecht wrote:

> Most of Mr. Harrison's poems are high-spirited romps, though perfectly contained within the metrical and stanzaic schemes he so clearly enjoys deploying. He is a poet who makes the most of his forms, which, together with an unusually versatile diction (as 'who can sing both high and low') keeps himself on his toes, and keeps his readers alert to every change in the linguistic topography he leads them through.

Hecht connected Harrison to Philip Hoy, founder of Waywiser Press, which published all his mature volumes, culminating in a *Collected Poems* that came out in April this year. With Hoy, Harrison launched Waywiser's Anthony Hecht Poetry Prize, which he managed since 2005, eventually becoming the press's Senior American Editor.

In a tribute to Bloom, who had taught the poet in his senior year at Yale, Harrison wrote about the liberating effects of anxiety-of-influence theory: 'I came to believe that the best way to deal with it was to go straight at it. If one is condemned to be a ventriloquist, one might as well embrace it.'

Harrison's four stand-alone volumes includes a *tour de force*, a feat of strophic ingenuity and generous wit. These poems have fun with canonical figures out of English and American letters: Shakespeare, Dr Johnson, Dickens, Whitman and Dickinson among them. Each book's title hints at the appropriation of other personae, literary or otherwise. (One is called *Identity Theft*; another, *Sometimes I Dream that I Am Not Walt Whitman*.) For all that, Harrison was no mere ventriloquist.

Revolutionary recoveries • *His long-time publisher New Directions writes of Jerome Rothenberg (1931–2024)*: We mourn the passing of our friend Jerome Rothenberg, a pivotal figure of contemporary American poetry. It is a loss to all who knew him and his beautiful work.

'I was Jerome Rothenberg's editor for most of his dozen or so books published by ND', Peter Glassgold (for decades the editor-in-chief of New Directions) said, 'starting with *Poland/1931*, back in 1974. I was drawn to his work from the start, and not only because he was among the most agreeable authors I worked with over the years. There was also this happy coincidence: there is a Rothenberg branch of my family. In the matter of ancestral concerns, Jerry and I were naturally simpatico. ND published only a small portion of Jerry's work, which was vast. His poetry was in direct line with those exuberant modernists of yesteryear, the likes of Apollinaire, Huidobro, Schwitters, and Tzara. His public readings were astonishing performances. I recall one that opened with a long, almost unbearable silence, broken at last by a prolonged, hair-raising shout. There might be music, props, and costumes, but never any sense of frivolous intent. His massive anthologies were nothing less than revolutionary recoveries. Without him the field of ethnopoetics – the study and translation of indigenous poetries worldwide and on their own terms – would not now exist. He was short in stature but, in intellect and of innovation, a giant.'

A country that no longer exists • *Eva Grubin writes:* Yvonne Green (1957–2024), British poet and long-time friend of Carcanet and this magazine, left us on 15 April. She was born in Finchley, London, of Bukharan-Jewish heritage, descended from those who left what is now part of Uzbekistan to flee Bolshevik persecution in the early twentieth century. Yvonne published her first pamphlet, *Boukhara*, in 2007. It won the Poetry Business 2007 Book & Pamphlet Competition. Her first full length collection, *The Assay* (Smith Doorstop Books), was published in 2010 and translated into Hebrew in 2013. It was followed by *Honoured*, a Winter 2015 Poetry Book Society Recommendation, in which she explored what it means to have come from a country and a community that no longer exist, in a collection examining identity and the meaning of home. *Jam and Jerusalem*, published in 2018, considers the human cost of war and includes a section of her translations of Semyon Izrailevich Lipkin's poems, foreshadowing her subsequent work *After Semyon Izrailevich Lipkin: 1911–2003* which was the PBS Translation Choice for Winter 2011. She continued to champion Lipkin's work, and in 2023, she published two substantial volumes: *A Close Reading of Fifty-Three Poems* and *Testimony* (the latter from his literary memoirs). In 2016, Yvonne's extended poem 'The Farhud: Baghdad's Shabu'ot 1st and 2nd June 1941' was read in the Israeli Knesset to commemorate the Iraqi pogrom bearing that name. Yvonne was poet-in-residence to the Global Foundation for the Elimination of Domestic Violence, convened two-monthly poetry groups, one at Hendon Library called 'Wall of Words' and the second at JW3, Europe's largest Jewish cultural centre, called 'Taking the Temperature', and conducted weekly online poetry courses attended by an international audience. *PN Review* published *Without Your Jews* in 2007 and *A Lawyer's Poem* in 2008. In 2010 a rare interview that she conducted with Louise Glück appeared in *PN Review*. Yvonne was an accomplished poet but also a lover and promoter of poetry. She embraced diverse cultural perspectives. She was an irreplaceable presence in the poetry world as a poet and advocate for poetry.

Rationality doesn't carry you all the way • *His publisher Jonathan Cape announced the death of John Burnside (1955–2024):* John was amongst the most acclaimed writers of his generation and published prolifically across many forms – chiefly as a poet, but also as a novelist, memoirist, writer of short stories and academic works – over a career spanning nearly forty years. He won the Geoffrey Faber Memorial Prize for *Feast Days* (1992), the Whitbread Poetry Award for *The Asylum Dance* (2000), the Saltire Book of the Year for *A Lie About My Father* (2006), and in 2011 won both the T.S. Eliot Prize and the Forward Poetry Prize for *Black Cat Bone*. He wrote regularly for a number of publications including [*PN Review*,] the *Guardian*, the *TLS*, the *London Review of Books* and the *New Yorker*. In 2023 he received the highly prestigious David Cohen Prize, awarded biennially in recognition of an author's entire body of work.

Born in Dunfermline in 1955, his early life was spent in Cowdenbeath and then Corby, Northamptonshire. After studies in English and European Literature at the Cambridgeshire College of Arts and Technology, he spent a number of years as an analyst and software engineer in the computer industry, returning to Fife in 1996 after a long period trying to live what he called 'a normal life' in suburban Surrey. This superficially 'rational' life, however, was beset by profound personal struggles that were to some great extent due to being the son of an abusive, alcoholic father, as detailed in the remarkable and haunting memoirs *A Lie About My Father* and *Waking Up in Toytown*. John's long-standing focus in his work was often on the irrational, not the rational – as he said in 2011: 'Having been, as it were, mad, and lived with horror which at that moment I completely believed in, I know that rationality doesn't carry you all the way. Irrationality interests me more than anything: sometimes it's very dangerous, but it can be incredibly beautiful.'

After publishing his first collection *The Hoop* in 1988 [with Carcanet Press, a fact omitted from most of his obituaries], he began to work with Robin Robertson. John said that this is when 'everything changed' for him, and they continued to work together up to the publication of John's most recent collection, *Ruin, Blossom*, in 2024. [...]

Having been a writer-in-residence at the University of Dundee, John became a professor in the School of English at the University of St Andrews, with a focus on creative writing, ecology and American poetry. His various lives as a poet, author and academic came together in his history of twentieth-century poetry, *The Music of Time* (2019).

Slow-moving nomad • *Peter Manson writes:* The poet, gardener and land artist Gerry Loose died suddenly in Rothesay on 30 April, aged seventy-six. A 'slow-moving nomad', Gerry was born in London, spoke with an Irish accent, and had lived in Spain, Morocco and, for many years, in Scotland. Early contact with the sound poet and publisher Bob Cobbing encouraged him to edit and hand-print his own 1970s magazine and little press, *byways*, publishing work by Cid Corman, Tom Raworth, Gael Turnbull and many others. His selected poems, *Printed on Water*, was published in 2007, and a new collection, *without title*, is due from Shearsman later this year.

Gerry was a lifelong anti-war activist, and many of his poems reflect on the presence of nuclear weapons and their apologists in the West of Scotland. The 2014 book *fault line* is founded on the disconnect between the beauty of the Gareloch and the technological and bureaucratic violence of the Faslane submarine base on its shore. Every poem is divided in two, as if against itself, by the geological symbol for a strike-slip fault. The unclassifiable, funny and ultimately furious *that person himself* (2009) follows the wanderings of a tricksterish human-dog-fox-coyote hybrid through the post-nuclear landscapes of the US desert and Japan. Dedicated to hibakusha, the Japanese survivors of nuclear bombing, the book recalls Gerry's visits to the Nevada and New Mexico test sites, and to Hiroshima and Nagasaki. One of these visits led to the gift to Scotland of a kaki tree, the offspring of a tree which survived the destruction of Nagasaki. It now grows in Glasgow's Botanic Gardens, where Gerry was writer-in-residence for three years, often collaborating with his partner, the artist, photographer and curator Morven Gregor.

Gerry's site-specific artwork includes 'Sanctuary' (2013), in Saari, Finland, a circle of spruce saplings planted so closely that their mature growth will block human (but not faunal and avian) access to the interior. On the edge of the circle, he placed a stone inscribed *sanctum sanctorum*, the Holy of Holies. Gerry was a rare poet who really understood the epigraphic: if your poem is literally carved in stone, it can afford to speak quietly, even anonymously.

Some of Gerry's strangest and most beautiful writing emerges from his fifty-year fascination with ogham, the 'Celtic tree alphabet' of the early medieval stone inscriptions of Ireland and Scotland. As collected in *The Great Book of the Woods* (2020), Gerry's ogham workings are 'expanded translations' of a unique kind, drawing on the treatises of early Irish poet-grammarians, on place names and the names of symbols (each ogham letter was traditionally associated with a particular tree), as well as on the features of the landscape in which the stone was raised. Every possible cue is used to find and create meaning in relation to these famously enigmatic and fragmentary texts, and each poem feels like an epitome of Gerry's life-work, a signifying fusion of stone, tree, language and place.

The exuberance of other people • *John McAuliffe writes:* A memorial for Martin Amis was held at St Martin-in-the-Fields on 10 June, just over a year after his death at the age of seventy-three. His friends and family celebrated his work, quoting from his essays, fiction and conversation. Poetry was part of Amis's resource as a writer. He liked to say that the Elizabethan lyric poem might be England's contribution to world civilization, and he delighted in quoting Auden, Larkin and others while teaching fiction in Manchester at the Centre for New Writing from 2007–2011. Poetry also featured in a number of the memorial speeches, with Ian McEwan recalling that he, Amis and others tried to work out which poet was most memorable, excluding Shakespeare, by reciting lines or their memory of lines of poetry. Who do you think was most remembered? he asked the gathered congregation.

Nick Laird read the poem Amis had chosen as his favourite for an Irish anthology, *Lifelines*. The choice was just as surprising as discovering that W.B. Yeats topped his and McEwan's memorability poll; Amis's favourite poem had been William Blake's 'Hear the Voice of the Bard', the introductory poem to *Songs of Experience*. Among the other speakers, the actor Bill Nighy read passages from the fiction (but not the ageless 'Career Move', the short story in which impoverished screenwriters resubmit their work to little magazines while poets quarrel over international rights with their agents...); Tina Brown remembered asking him to review a David Hare play and Amis's response, 'Do I have to see it?' – theatre was not his preferred night out; James Fenton told a long, sidewinding story about the cartoonist Mark Boxer whose punchline seemed to go missing somewhere around Oxford; Zadie Smith remembered meeting him first as a student fan and then a New York dinner companion, and her continuing, almost Leavisite conviction that his were novels in which *life* itself still counted; the other speakers were his wife Isabel, and three of his children, Delilah and Fernanda, and Louis who, catching the delight that characterized the novels' propulsive rhythms, remembered that his father's 'favourite thing in life, off the page, was witnessing the exuberance of other people'.

Reports

Fragments on Fragments: Singing Vessels

ANTHONY VAHNI CAPILDEO

Almost two hundred years ago, in 1832, Percy Bysshe Shelley, in 'With a Guitar, To Jane', speaks in the voice of Ariel, the airy sprite from Shakespeare's *Tempest.* Shelley's Ariel claims to have served Miranda and her father Prospero faithfully, only to be rewarded with solitude or imprisonment, and forgotten. Therefore, with the boundaryless illogic of passionate submission, Ariel presents Miranda with a gift. Ariel is a fool for love. Shelley, in ninety-one lines like one deep exhalation, presents us twice with the word 'love'. The 'silent token' of Ariel's devotion is a 'loved Guitar', loved by the luthier who made it. The last line assures Miranda, Jane, the troubadour's lady, the person to whom you read this poem aloud, that it will reserve its finest music 'For one beloved Friend alone'. The lover, or poem, has been wrought with sharp tools into a musical instrument.

Playable by many, to any air they choose, the lover, or poem, nonetheless promises a certain kind of exclusivity. The lyric of swoon and glow, that we freely rehearse, secretly has one and only one recipient, and one and only sender. 'With a Guitar, To Jane', belongs in concert to that servant-sender and adored recipient. We catch an echo of a thrill built up of unutterable and unequal experience, some shared, some separate. Unusually, Ariel flashes back to the felling of the tree from which the guitar was crafted, and thence to the harmonious ecology of the trees murmuring their praise and love in tune with the natural/created world. By dying to its tree-identity, losing its tree-companions, and giving up its tree-respiration, the tree-material is reborn into a musical and emotional ecosystem of human body and breath.

The guitar is a curvy shape that warms up and yields its voice as it is hugged to a human body that can pluck, strike, stroke, tingle and strum. Federico García Lorca plays on this early in his poetic tragedy of small-town repression, *La Casa de Bernarda Alba*, where enclosed women gossip about a loose woman who lets herself be carried away on horseback by a man who holds her as if he were playing the guitar. With this image, Lorca both conveys the bitter and snippy tone of sexual yearning mixed with judgmentalism and fear, and sets a kind of imaginary background music thrumming, one made of night and a woman returning herself to the woods. As a pre-internet era child in a country with few music shops, to learn musical technique I listened to pirated recordings of the classical guitarist Andrés Segovia. He taught shamelessness. His interpretations were romantic in their *tempo rubato* approach, where 'robbed' time hurries or sways around the prescribed measure. They were erotic in their audible breath and the squeak of finger-contact with the neck and strings. Nothing too clean here.

Forget eros, as I like to do. Cradling and singing is also how humans like to care for their young. When Holly Pester invited me to take part in her *Common Rest* research and improvisation, which resulted in a seven-track album (Prototype, 2016) of her collaborations with poets, she was investigating the sounds and rhythms of labour, work, nurturance, care, rest. We had a box of natural and manufactured objects to make sounds with. We cradled strings of shells and bells and other things, rocking and crooning. Somehow the speed picked up. We were shaking our object-babies to death, in a frenzy of improvised cries. This is what happens when poets are left in the dark. Recalling the sea and our different childhood coastlines, connected by the warm Gulf Stream transoceanic current, a little horrified at how quickly the maternal shades into the mænadic, we slowed things down, Holly vocalizing, I playing the innards of a piano like a harp. We left acceleration behind for a reposeful back-and-forth that the sound engineers would make into a shimmer playing over depth. If we were saints in the Roman Catholic tradition, those Wellcome Trust props, cardboard box, tambourines and all, would now be contact relics.

What are 'contact relics'? They are items that have been touched by a saint during their lifetime: for example, clothing, or prayer beads; or presumably, musical instruments. As Jordan Scott OP reminds us, relics are 'heavenly signposts' that make us think beyond this world. They are not magical. Just as the person in their life on earth was a temple of the Holy Spirit, fragments of their self or things they used may become conduits now that they are living in heaven. In a sense, relics are not macabre, pertaining to the dead, but allow us to touch eternity, to feel continuity with a beloved friend. This is like, but not the same as, the shiver of time and presence we may feel on hearing someone singing and playing James Joyce's guitar as part of the Dún Laoghaire sound map project. I wonder whether entire places can be 'contact relics', of a sort. Say, the cell where the imprisoned St Cuthbert Mayne may have sung and must have prayed, in Launceston Castle. Are these now 'resonant places', rather than 'thin places'? Are we open to being re-tuned, if we put ourselves in these places, contemplate their past contact with some beloved and, if only with our breathing, add to their activation by sound?

This is why visiting St Margaret Clitherow's relic in the Bar Convent, York, listening into its surroundings, and whispering back, has become an important part of my creative process as Writer in Residence. It is, however, a corporeal relic, not a contact relic. The hand from the musical instrument of the body, not the body of the wooden instrument made to sing. When I saw her hand, I had no words for its delicacy. The enchantment of the diminutive is missing from English, except in the cuteness and corruption of internet speech. In my teens, I learnt to enjoy reading the apparatus of English translations of Russian novels for the explanatory notes on the variations of naming and the untranslatability of the inflections of tenderness. Tenderness is untranslatable; it does not carry over perfectly; it is the water spilled on the grass by an anxious speech-bearer. Diminutives, charmingly, can make a word or name longer. Translate petting a creature into respelling: 'dog' as 'doggg'. The spelling-pronunciation of 'doggggg' tails off heavily, sounding as stupid as it looks. The rightful vocabulary of fools for love.

At first, I thought that St Margaret's hand was covered by a dainty lace glove. No. That was her skin. She is thirty years old, but it was four hundred and thirty-eight years ago that she was pressed to death under rocks and sharp stones in the city of York. Her crime was to shelter Roman Catholic priests in the mid-1500s, one of those colourful eras that we prefer to remember through the artwashing of costume drama, while decrying archival research as wokery. This tiny hand is quite plain. Not dramatic. Not dusty. You won't be Tudorpilled. 'Margaret' means 'pearl', and 'marguerite' translates as 'daisy'. These associations fit like a glove.

If you are seeing the hand, that means you, or someone, has drawn back the rich, sober curtain that covers the glassed wall where the relic sits meekly but upward-stretching, like a lone candle-flame. Secrecy, for the sake of survival, is part of the fabric of the Bar Convent, which, dating from 1686, is perhaps the oldest surviving such foundation in continuous active use. The chapel is built on purpose like a private ballroom or family theatre. The secret worshippers, for survival, at any moment could become players, pretending to be at an entertainment, while the holy servers and the evidence of their service disappeared rapidly through many exits and entrances, through concealed doors and under floors. You can sit or kneel, very still, and keep the hand company, in awareness of the knife-edge where fellowship and the criminalization of fellowship trembled.

I thought of St Margaret's delicate hand when I saw the man cradling the child, crying out a chant or song over and over, and dancing. Was he celebrating survival? There was a bloody bandage over the child's eyes; the perfect little one blinded, but full of future, love, and even happiness. I then learnt that the child had been alive, blinded, but subsequently had its head blown off. His father, with a fixed expression like a smile, and unblinking eyes, was dancing the baby, dancing the baby, lullaby and lament in one. Then it occurred to me that, in the martyrdom of his people, there would be few corporeal or contact relics. Palestine itself is becoming a collective 'contact relic', an un-sanctuary, a thinned place. There is boundaryless illogic in pretending that 'politics' and the lyrical are not in collision. This is the musical and emotional ecosystem of human body and breath into which writers and audiences have been co-opted. But the festivals must go on.

Set 5: Mondo de Sunbrilo

TRANSLATED BY JOHN GALLAS

1

Complaint   *Hans Davidsohn (Jakob van Hoddis) (1887-1942)/Jewish-Germany*

And will the sunlight murder all my dreams –
the pale, sweet children of my lazy fancies?
The days have got so garish and so flat.
My satisfaction wears a cloudy hat.
Anxieties disturb my peace.

Like Celestial-Solar Police.

2

Cockadoodledoo   *(Anon/first century B.C./China)*

In the east the sun is shouldering near. The stars' sparkle fades.
The cock stalks up the wall and shrieks. Cockadoodledoo!
Last night's songs are done, the waterclock has run out,
the remains of a party lie scattered in the dining room.
The moon politely dissolves with the stars. Morning is here.
Click clack at a thousand gates and ten thousand doors
the keys, like little flipping fish, turn in their wards.
Round the Big House, and up by the fortress
the crows and magpies take up the new, bright air.

3

Oarplash   *(Guþmundur Magnússon (1873–1918)/Iceland)*

Slow and steady comes the morning,
Clouds belt on their straps of light,
A high moon dwindles on the moors,
The lit sea stirs now, tangle-bright.
Now the mane-waves' rippled spray
Gleams in widening strakes, and then –
the plashy dip and take of oars,
as men strike out to face the day.

4
Sunrise *(Anon/Gabon)*

Dead darkness trips over
& falls headlong
at your flashlight glare...

your beamy eye-arrows
shot from your firebox...

flare-broadside
that rips its coat
the pitch-coat stitched with starstuds...

yes yes your flareshots
rip the pitch-coat with a glare...

5
A seaday with fishingboats *(Anon/St Lucia)*

masts – loose paddles – hulls – clack & rattle –
lemon-lit – & sunrise shines the fishboats'
insect-oars – pricking the sealine – burst with light –
the sky behind a yellow door – & smaller still –
& smaller still –

& day stands like the unstirred air
inside a house –

midday – & the sea lies alone – straight as a windowledge –
straight as a swept floor –

evening – & the sky reds alone – full as a windowblind –
full as a wood wall –

masts – loose paddles – hulls – clack & rattle –
the land waits for the insect-boats –
the sea has no backdoor –

Notes:

1. Complaint – new
2. Cockadoodledoo – new
3. Oarplash – new
4. Sunrise – from 'The Song Atlas' (some small changes)
5. A seaday with fishingboats – from 'The Song Atlas'
   (some small changes)

On a New Blue Poet's Plaque

MICHAEL SCHMIDT

I attended Joy Scovell's funeral at Oxford Crematorium in the company of Anne Ridler, who had introduced me to her over a decade before. In the front row I remember three of her sisters, some older (she had been well into her nineties). What a stalwart family it seemed, and how together! At the end we sang 'The day thou gavest, Lord, is ended', and parts of Psalm 103. Robert Elton offered a family tribute. Theresa Frayn spoke of the poet, Katie Buffonge read a poem of Joy's, and Wilma Elton read Tennyson's 'Crossing the Bar'. Literary tributes came from the novelist Maggie Gee and from me, her publisher.

That event on 30 December 1999, millennium end, was a celebration. The blue plaque event twenty-five years later was even more of a celebration as the poet and her husband were recalled, their home marked for posterity. I know that Joy's poems have a posterity. It is not a popular posterity, she won't become a set text. It is a presence that single readers will happen upon in anthologies and follow up: her singular poems let us in to a unique and unexpected imagination, timeless in its concerns, deft in its forms, an imagination rooted in a tradition which survives despite changes in fashion. We know her as a translator but especially, to use the words of that severest twentieth-century critic and anthologist Geoffrey Grigson, 'a poet less concerned with celebrity and self-importance than with being alive and in love'. She is, he added, 'the purest woman poet of our time'. I think we can drop the word 'woman': Grigson's statement retains its force without that hint of condescension.

I fell in love with Joy's poems when I read a pamphlet published by Peter Scupham and John Mole of the Mandeville Press, *Listening to Collared Doves*. The title poem begins 'I am homesick now for middle age, as then / For youth', and accepts that 'our natural span may be enough'. She is a poet of and for maturity, for adult readers. Her poems keep open ways back to childhood, youth and middle age, and accept what Philip Larkin coldly

calls 'age, and then the only end of age'. I appreciate her more each year.

She contributed eight times to *PNR*, beginning in 1988 with a collection of her distinctive Giovanni Pascoli translations. Her later contributions were poems and an interview with Jem Poster in 1990. The last of her poems printed in *PNR* came in 1995, almost thirty years ago. One of these last poems was 'A Snowfall'.

> In this temperate climate, in the Thames valley,
> Under our cloudy skies the snow comes rarely
> Unlooked-for, in the dark, beyond belief
> Like visitings of angels and as brief.
>
> Their wings are white over roofs, their luminous
> Hands bring to light the fine bones of the trees.
> Something we apprehend, not ours to possess,
> Say beauty itself, they inhabit a while for us,
>
> And by noon are gone, unless a feather flutters
> Here and there darkening in the rainy gutters.

Another poem seemed especially apposite for the unveiling of the plaque, for the house itself, and for its conjuring the poet, her family and by extension our own ghosts, comfortable and uncomfortable, present, past and to come.

> The days of our ghosthood were these;
> When we were children, when we had no keys
> We entered through closed doors, unseen went
>   out again.
> Our souls were the dissolved, ungathered,
>   filtering rain.
> Our bodies sat upon our parents' knees.
>
> In the second days of our ghosthood
> We went on foot among a multitude,
> In time of drought. In our hard youth, we
>   winter-born.
> And those were visible to men as flowers in
>   corn
> Whose souls were eyes unseen that gaze from
>   dark.
>
> We entered flesh and took our veil, our state.
> The third days of our ghosthood wait.
> When we are stripped by pain, by coming death
>   far-seen,
> Of earthly loves, earth's fruit, that came so late
>   to hand,
> With that waking or falling into dream
> We shall not cross into an unfamiliar land.

Letter from Wales

SAM ADAMS

When I learned that the novelist J.L. Carr was christened Joseph Lloyd, I assumed a Welsh family connection. Later discovery that he was born in 1912 persuaded me otherwise. His parents were solidly Yorkshire, Joseph his father's name, and Lloyd in all likelihood an indication of liberal-leaning politics and a salute to Lloyd George, then famed as a great reforming Chancellor of the Exchequer. In any case, and for reasons unfathomable, the writer preferred to be known as 'Jim'. Yet there is a link to Wales in his writing. I have been reading *A Month in the Country* – again, for I feel the need to pick it off the shelf once or twice a year. It's a short read, leaving one wanting more, yet always strangely satisfying. The book ends with a brief note of where and when, his tale told, Carr laid down his pen: *Stocken, Presteigne, September 1978.* Presteigne (its Welsh name, *Llanandras*, meaning the church of Saint Andrew) is no doubt the postal address of Stocken Farm, just over a mile to the north of the town centre, and at that point fifty yards or less from the Welsh border. Some of its land is quite possibly in Powys, *our* side, as is Presteigne. Powys is Wales's largest county in area, its smallest in terms of population. For a time I had responsibilities there that entailed driving upwards of twenty thousand miles a year. Most of the roads were, and probably still are, narrow, but traffic was always light, often absent. I confess that on occasion, travelling between destinations on the moorland east of Llandrindod Wells, given a fine day, I would stop the car and get out for a breath of air. This is the part of Wales known as the 'Green Desert', and it was wonderful in those brief halts to hear the high mewing of buzzards overhead and look up to see them circling slowly, broad wings spread.

Carr's son, Bob, recalled camping holidays thereabouts, and other clues suggest the border area a couple of hours or so almost due west of home in Kettering was a favourite destination. Though formerly the county town of Radnorshire, with even now fewer than three thousand inhabitants, Presteigne is no bustling metropolis, but it has roots going back at least as far as 1262, when it was besieged by Llywelyn ap Gruffydd, the last true Prince of Wales. This is the sort of detail that attracted Carr, who probably found his way to the Radnorshire Arms, a timber-framed early seventeenth-century hostelry in the High Street. It would have appealed to his heightened sense of the history of place, and it was a short stroll from his base at Stocken Farm. I like to think that, settled comfortably in the pub lounge with a pint for company and no distracting hubbub, he added a few lines to his story. These days we can summon up witnesses to the time he spent at the farm: a former owner recalled the man 'who stayed in their orchard' and had given his family a copy of the elaborate map of Herefordshire he had made on which he inserted by hand a sketch of the farmhouse.

The stimulus for this foray into the historically blurred border zone of Wales and England is Byron Rogers's biography of Carr, *The Last Englishman,* which I should have read long ago. *The Man Who Went into the West*, the biography of R.S. Thomas that brought Rogers the James Tait Black Memorial Prize, I did read almost as soon as it came out, with admiration and, it must be admitted, envy. As I have mentioned before, I met R.S. in Aberystwyth in 1956, when he gave a singularly unimpressive talk about poetic imagery to UCW English Society, without once mentioning he had ever written a poem. It was a rare opportunity to engage with the then famously reticent poet, but I lacked the journalistic skill, or common sense, decency perhaps, to engage him in conversation, give him the chance to open up. He did just that (to a degree) later, and Byron Rogers clearly had the companionable qualities of the astute questioner and good listener. His essentially informal full-length portrait of the poet is unlikely to be superseded.

There was a period when 'Anglo-Welsh' writers would gather for conferences, readings and bus trips to places with literary associations, the *Academi Gymreig* organising events from its Arts Council funded office in Cardiff. Members came from all parts of Wales and from as far afield as London for these occasions. If anything of the kind is happening now, I haven't been told about it. Were it still flourishing, I wonder whether Rogers, who initially established himself as a Fleet Street feature writer, would have become a member and joined in. He and I have at least one thing in common: we both went up to Aberystwyth at seventeen. However, one year was enough for him and he abandoned Professor Gwyn Jones and long Saturday morning sessions of *Beowulf* in the book-lined, round tower room at *y coleg ger y lli* for Oxford. He doesn't dwell on his translation to that far older, revered seat of learning, but clearly it was not through family influence or money. He was born into the Welsh-speaking working class at Bancyfelin, Carmarthenshire, his father a gifted joiner-woodworker. In *Me – The Authorised Biography* he describes himself self-deprecatingly: 'the scholarship boy, showy, shallow, knowing exactly what would please the various examining boards at which I was pointed, but little else'. Higher education set him up for a career different from the traditional Welsh route into or via teaching. An attempt at a historical novel about Owain Glyndwr having foundered, despite encouragement from J.L. Carr, he had accumulated thirty years' experience in journalism, including a stint as speech writer for the then Prince Charles (he would turn up at Buckingham Palace on a bicycle), before, nearing sixty, in 2001 he published his first book, *An Audience with an Elephant*, a collection of previously written articles. In book form he is an engaging, entertaining, thought provoking essayist: 'The Lost Children', about the life and death in captivity at Sempringham Abbey in Lincolnshire of Gwenllian, the daughter of Prince Llywelyn, was republished in a fine edition by Gwasg Gregynog in 2005, a rare accolade. His own story, *Me*, is full of extraordinary characters, and he writes with rare candour about relationships with family and friends, not flinching at the truths of later life. Towards the end he tells of his foray into marketing, with his own book. Bookshops, Waterstones and the rest, will have nothing to do with it. He confides this to his local butcher, who volunteers space for a pile alongside the Paxo. The author points out that there ought to be some return for the butcher and proposes a free pound of sausages at his expense with each book. This story spread from the local newspaper to the national broadsheets, radio and television. It was, Rogers observes, a lesson in the value of publicity.

Features

Spiderings

GWYNETH LEWIS

1

Spider Mother

In that top corner, my torch picks out
the eight red eyes of one cunning spider,

wedged like a camera in its nest of wires.
I am the mote in each eye. Her gazes

trap me, like weighted nets
which have taken me down more times

than I care to admit. Once I'm felled,
down she abseils and crawls

tickling, into my ear, to lay eggs
into my brain. Those cells adjust

to their guest with seasons of migraine
through which I rest, until she emerges,

triumphant, through the arch of my mouth,
clad in chainmail of living armour:

glittering spiderlings, hatched from my mind –
if that can be called my own now, or home.

2

Spider's Cage

I won't call her spider,
                        though I do.
I live in the cage of her legs.
                        I've speared
my heart on a pointed stick to attract
                        carnivorous angels
which make a great racket of wings
                        but can't save.
'It's easy to leave, what stops you?'
                        others ask, baffled.
It's the snare in the brain, spring-loaded
                        for suicide. The knots
throb, tighten, anguish swells
                        till the trigeminal
nerve slithers out – a hot, pulsing snake –
                        through my eyeball,
leaving a spider's web tattooed
                        on my face
like a shattered windscreen.
                        This pattern alarms
employers but, honest, though I tell
                        of such horrors,
underneath, I'm a bit of a sweetie.

3

Maze

First, locate your original wound.
I come to in the bathroom, a body beside
me. Did we? Could I have? Check between legs
for dampness. Next, torso. Is this
my own blood? If not, then whose?

Tied to my hand is a thread of scarlet,
zinging. Lose it, I die. So I follow its pull
through this maze and its generations,
a crazed enfilade of dead ends, cluttered
box rooms. Outside, huge thud, as a gull etc
while, outside – huge thud, a gull

flies into a window. The bird is shattered
in three: the flesh one slides down but its shadow
veers off at an angle, climbs, clicking sun's shutter
right in my face, and the third is a burglar alarm
wailing, 'Emergency!'. Which one should I follow?

4

Missing

So, did I give my luck away? For piano
exams and degrees I wore a chain
with a silver spider plucking death
like a tune on her web, but in my favour.
I passed – how fortunate! My mother
'keep it safe', but now I want it.

No sign in the shoebox filled with Whitby jet
in tissue paper, moss agate brooches and –
swift recoil – underneath, a foetus mother
made from my nerves, nourished by ichor,
sour as wasp soup. She mewls for attention.
Too late. On me, her charm's broken.

I'll knit my own token instead: fling a cable
formed from habits of mind and the skill
of not being me for a while over the chasm.
Once it's slung, I'll test the tension,
step out, eyes fixed on the other side,
to dance its wide road, with my parasol.

5

Not my doll, but just like her

I never loved mine, Siwan Elin: I opened
her clock face, its movement stopped dead,
clogged up with dead spiders. She told
the wrong time because we were trapped
in rooms snowed under by dead-skin blizzards.

Round here skips mark out the ongoing massacre
of parents, each one a Pompeii. A hand sticks out
in appeal from a luggage landslide, I rescue a blonde
dolly: hand-knitted pinafore in sage, matching
knickers and vest. Who says you can't choose

your own household gods? My lares
protector had been repaired
with elastic, holding head, torso, limbs
together. That perished, she fell apart,
so I'm forced to dispose of more body parts.

6

Any Eight Legs Will Do

I order a dress online: the design
is a blazon of giant arachnids, rampant –
emblems of terror tamed into fashion.
The Chinese wove spiders' thread
into luxury fabric, but gossamer
tears, like metaphor.

The man who hands over my dress
has a forearm tattoo: a four-masted schooner –
full press of sails – attacked by Kraken.
The rigging frays, sailors fall
from shrouds into roiling
water, strakes part like lace –
and DOWN
goes the ship,
me with her,
mutating...

jellyfish brush past my leg,
light as lost breath...
tentacles twine, suckers
taste nipples, vulva...
we sink together...
I'm calm in my
monster's arms...

one flesh, we blush
iridescent with dreams
and, flushing,
I'm undone
at the seams

7

Spidering

Now comes the mind-blinding fall
through thin air, the hissing spool
of silk high above me, a rope
that could hang me. I've anchored my web,

so pay out a loop, repeat, to form
a billowing compass rose
then listen, intently through outspread feet
for something to fall. Queen Jezebel

was flung by eunuchs from the palace window
onto the flagstones below, trampled
by horses, dog-savaged, till all that was left
were her palms, soles and skull.

Next I perceive the queen's physical rhyme:
a run-over vole on a lane, left paw-pads
still perfect, held up, in vain, to deflect the tyre,
her torso crushed to a hand-pressed flower

of fur, exquisite. Then, something between
the two, I haul myself in. I neither survived
King Jehu's triumph nor the juggernaut wheel but –
don't ask me how, I'm still feeling, pulling.

8

Away!

A decade ago, I fell down a crevasse
and froze, while overhead passed

climbers in thousands on rickety ladders
chatting, making less sense than the stars.

Beneath them, my frost-bitten heart was their anchor,
though they didn't know it. Now sherpas

have found me. They resemble their fathers,
but taller; they lead me gently to unfurl

my prayer-flags, raising my arms in thanks,
but I've lived so long now on so little

that the merest wisp of a thermal
pulls me aloft, a stitch dropped

but picket up again. I'm not alone:
around me are thousands ballooning

and, glinting from each self-suffering chain,
the star of a spider diamond.

Principalities, Dominions

I copy a Chalcid Wasp from a diagram,
admire it, an insect cherubim,

four wings and forelegs all raised in praise,
as if grace falls like rain in this paper's grain.

'Holy! Holy! Holy!' Evangelical, it sings,
and I take care of the scimitar sting

of adrenaline over my heart. Wasps feed on flies,
spiders and ticks, which they keep alive

while gorging. So, am I eaten or eater? Important
to know. I'm neither and both — for 'Providence...

keep[s] every animal in check by some other... more
powerful'* (see overleaf). Do you dare turn over?

*Quoted in A.D. Imms, *Insect Natural History* (The New Naturalist series, Collins, 1947, p. 127)

Gwyneth Lewis

In Conversation with Alice Entwistle

In some ways Nightshade Mother, *your new prose book, is heartbreaking. Somewhere you say that writing it is killing you, and the reader knows exactly what you mean. But elsewhere you explain how language gives you the resources to do the job. How did the whole thing come about?*

I've been planning this book since I was in my early twenties but, despite having written about a tough subject, depression, before, nothing could have prepared me for the difficulties of this task. Part of the emotional abuse I suffered at my mother's hands involved her hijacking my writing at an early age, so the subject was like turning the knife I'd been wounded with back on myself again.

I've always trusted form to shield me from explosive subjects, so I was surprised to find that, in writing the first draft of this book, I'd retraumatized myself and felt suicidal. I hadn't allowed myself to look at the full extent of the abuse before and it was worse than I'd realised. So, initially, the writing was the opposite of therapeutic and required a lot of raging and grieving. However, with the final version, I'm finding relief in getting the story out of my body and into the world.

I spent years writing of elaborate techniques that *implied* what happened without spelling it out. I worked out overall schemes, involving tarot cards and various metaphors, such as James Tilly Matthews's 'Air Loom', until eventually I found that I could use text – letters, diaries – as a way through the story. I'm very distrustful of emotion on its own and intuited that I had to provide evidence for what I'm asserting, not because I'm not telling the truth but because it's really important to test my own sense of rage and injustice against what can be shown to have happened. This is the result of having been gaslit for decades: I had to follow the evidence trail to convince myself that this was not just a matter of me being 'difficult'. In family conflicts I was often described as being 'dramatic' or 'over-sensitive', as if I were the problem.

I can understand the compulsion to check and recheck (you've always seemed a scholarly writer although you wear it lightly); and vindication brings relief, doesn't it? In the book you describe the feeling of 'release'. You are wary of mistaking writing for therapy; could we think of it as cauterizing, perhaps, more than cathartic?

Because I was abused by someone who disregarded fairness and was swept away on raw emotion, I've developed a holy fear of using feelings as a basis for action – I've seen how badly it can deceive a person. I didn't want to become like my mother, whom I hated when she behaved towards me in that way, but also because it's wrong and causes such damage. Not that emotion is bad. There is a form of deep feeling that's modulated by moral thinking, exercised over time and with discernment, that I trust.

I did write a doctorate but this book is more forensic. An abused person has been forcibly knocked off their own axis, deprived of the capacity to know intuitively what they think. I have to work very hard to establish that and poetry has been an invaluable tool in the process, because it's not coercive, it rewards exploration and failure; the ability to change your mind is built into the form.

I've no doubt that I'm better off psychologically for practising the art. But no medium is benign in itself. It's easy to be pushed into sentiments you don't mean and into structures of thought that are pre-determined by linguistic bias. Look what the syntax of Artificial Intelligence is producing from the discourse of social media. The algorithms drive us into things we don't want to say, like rats in a maze. Writing good poetry is a balance between allowing yourself to be carried away by language and refusing to be pushed around by it. I'm aware all the time of choosing to exercise free will in my poems, because being carried away by the language melody is the equivalent of unthinking emotion. Something which sounds good doesn't mean that it is so. And yet, the music can be a clue to something worthwhile happening. It's like the dialogue between a horse and rider, with both as equal partners.

As you explain, the toxicity of your 'mother tongue' made bilingualism into a 'fissure', impossible to navigate safely. Over the years, you've occasionally hinted that your poems were encoding sensitive materials. But as an English teacher Eryl was a confident and skilful poetry reader; did she ever spot herself?

I've always thought that the metaphor of a 'mother tongue' should be interrogated for its shadow side, especially because Welsh cultural nationalism draws on the mother as an entirely benign figure. Like flesh-and-blood mothers, culture isn't always benign. In a healthy debate, unacknowledged exclusions and fantasies need to be called out.

I've been exploring my home situation all my writing life, in code. This is more and less explicit in various places and some shrewd critics have noticed it. Eryl certainly did and made her resentment and disapproval known to me. Having written *Nightshade Mother*, I'm much less inhibited, as 'Spiderings' shows. Perhaps that's been the main payoff of facing an internal taboo, the freedom to go for broke.

You say 'Aesthetics are at the core of the relationship between my mother and me'. Perhaps the book 'disentangles' nothing more thoroughly than the creativity which binds and divides you.

My mother was a talented writer and, had she been able to develop and realise that practice, would have been a much happier person. My literary tastes, of course, were formed by her from childhood – we both loved Milton, for example – but once I rebelled in terms of writing, she lost interest in poetry. What I meant about the aesthet-

ics being central to our relationship has more to do with how abuse affects a child. Despite knowing no other upbringing, I could never fully 'believe' my parents were behaving in such cruel ways. This means that I had the model for another way of being somewhere in my mind. Trying to establish a healthy relationship with my parents was like failing to revise a bad poem. Some projects have to be abandoned.

Reading models alternative ways of being, especially for kids. Did reading help you write the book?

I can't separate reading from writing: they both require an act of imagination, negotiated through language, which signals a willingness to have your mind changed and an invitation to transcend your own limitations. I was a very fast reader when I was younger; I now allow myself to be deliberate, thinking hard about the implications of what I read and how an author has approached a subject, and what the style says. I take notes, which infuriates me, but I know it's the best way for me to retain what I've read.

Discussions of maternal cruelty are so rare, it must have felt lonely. Did you confide in anyone?

No, I told hardly anybody and if I did, it was in strict confidence. When I began thinking of writing the book, I was still feeling deep shame about the experience, and I knew I could only do the work in secret, until I had a full first draft. There were many false starts, but the reactions of a very few trusted readers made a huge difference to the final version. When I was finally able to talk to a couple of women who'd been abused by their mothers, the relief was life-changing because they understood how fundamental an attack it is on the self and how hard you have to fight to gain any solid ground. Their companionship, found late, is hugely important to me.

I looked everywhere I could for books on the subject. In poetry, alice hiller's *bird of winter* is notable; likewise Vivian Gornick's prose work *Fierce Attachments*. I couldn't see anything like the account I thought I could write, so that was an incentive.

A new collection – First Rain in Paradise – *is due from Bloodaxe next March. Did those poems emerge with* Nightshade Mother*? Or afterwards?*

I could never have written such explicit poems before the memoir. I started the poems after the first draft of the memoir, as part of *The Poetry Detective: Reading and Writing Past Fear*, a critical book being published by Princeton next year. In teaching, I've devised a way of getting writers and readers past their terror of saying what they mean; I drafted 'Spiderings' as samples of how to get difficult ideas down on the page in various ways, building up to a sequence. I'm half-appalled and half-delighted with this new lack of inhibition; they will form a key section of the new collection.

That spider metaphor summons Eryl-as-maker – the clothes, the dolls, the cakes; and also the ghastly lisping giant arachnid Penelope in A Hospital Odyssey, *which as an arachnophobe I've not forgotten...*

Ah, you see, I did let the spider have her say in *A Hospital Odyssey*! So now it's my turn... though, of course, it's all my imaginative construction.

Going back to the memoir, amid the emotion and hostility, the snatches of dialogue with Mwnci, a childhood toy, puncture and retune key moments in the psychodrama. It's very deft. Mwnci made me think of the ventriloquist Nina Conti, and her rather tyrannical monkey. Was your Mwnci always an ally?

Yes, I know Nina Conti's work; I love her Monkey because he's so rude to her. When I found an old glove puppet of a monkey in the attic while we were clearing my parents' house, my body recognized him. I knew immediately that I had loved him and still do. I was never keen on dolls but Mwnci was different enough to be sympathetic. If you've been gaslit, the greatest difficulty of writing the family story from your point of view is that you get dragged back into the version that was forced on you, no matter how much you resist. Writing *Nightshade Mother*, I tried desperately to find a voice of last resort in myself that I could trust. Mwnci speaks from the primitive brain, the deep body; using his persona, I could say things that I was too frightened to utter in my own persona. He shares many characteristics with Leighton, my husband: he's very forthright, funny and, most important, on my side, but not uncritically.

Then there's your aunt Megan and your uncle Bill; simply reading about their home in Illinois felt somehow restorative. I know you made regular visits but geographically they must have seemed out of reach. Was there any support nearer home?

In the 1970s and 1980s there was nowhere to turn to for help. The SSRIs were decades away; access to therapy today is much easier. There was some pastoral care at school but the teachers were my mother's friends and colleagues. Plus, over-performing students like me were assumed to be fine. In fact, it's part of the camouflage – you do well in order to stay out of trouble at home. I couldn't tell my friends because, in a small community, secrets are buried deep. The closest I had to surrogate mothers were people like my very eccentric ballet teacher, Joyce Marriott, who at least could see me artistically. I once told her I was thinking of going into the law and she told me not to be ridiculous, I was far too creative. But these were crumbs. So, yes, it was lonely. The whole experience has left me with a strong suspicion of groups, like families, unless they allow you the maximum possible degree of free will.

My actual mother was so difficult that I've never wanted a surrogate for her, the whole model was – and is – too painful to deal with. I'd much rather have a dog.

You've described the paralysis of not knowing how to understand a situation except by filtering it through someone else's view of it; of losing the capacity for self-knowledge in

childhood. Opening your story to scrutiny seems terribly risky. Do you fear publication?

You've understood the dilemma perfectly and yes, it is risky to publish. Parts of the writing process left me suicidal, though I'm a long way from that now. I've got support systems in place, but I know that I'm vulnerable. However, having written this story to the best of my ability has left me feeling a confidence I haven't had before and another body – the book – between me and the formative experiences of childhood. In this sense, writing can change you at a cellular level.

While it's certainly true that I've been knocked out of my own centre, there is a paradoxical payoff to being gaslit: being forced to experience another person's emotional trajectory gives you a kind of cognitive bilingualism. But it risks obliterating your own view, which is disastrous. I do see other people's points of view easily, even when they're arguing against me, but that's preferable to a monovision which traps you in your own realm of regard. It's a basis for empathy, at least. I'm not saying that there's anything good about being emotionally abused. It has left me very resilient, although I would much rather have been better parented.

You depict the whole process as a kind of agonizing auto-immunization. This recalls both the memoir's botanical frame, and the herbarium Eryl and you made together. But your book exposes other properties in the medicinal plants in Nicholas Culpeper's Complete Herbal.

I wrote *Nightshade Mother* primarily to understand the shape of what had happened to me; both the narrative of my childhood, and its distorting effects on my mind and body. This, I feel, is something that can be shared with others who've suffered from the same problem. In this project, metaphor has been key, because it allows you to traverse time and space to create a momentary foothold. It crumbles soon enough but each image is a stepping stone. I did want an overall image, so that people would know what the book is, namely a taxonomy of being both nourished and poisoned by the same person. The image also had the virtue of arising naturally from the story of what Eryl and I did together; our herbarium gave me great pleasure and a lifelong interest in identifying and understanding plants.

The word 'toxic', much-bandied about in psycho-babble these days, describes very accurately how mental illness and distress feel. Your system is compromised: it can't right itself or administer its own medicine. That has to come from the outside (somatic therapy has been crucial for me). The concept of poisoning carries its own hope, though, in the idea of an antidote, even while the one required in this situation is very hard to come by and different for everybody. For me, it's in noticing more, being precise, honest and facing the full impact and complexity of my family situation. Then there's the rest of the world to attend to, equally mixed, difficult but also full of glories.

I know what possibilities I've lost because I was damaged by emotional abuse; other people's self-confidence amazes and baffles me. But, along with having been poisoned (and I have to adjust to that daily), I'm also delighted by the vividness of the life and loving that have come my way.

I'm realizing that I wanted to read your metaphors as a constellation illuminating different angles of the experiences you describe, but they wouldn't always connect for me, and now I understand why. Seeing them as stepping stones, leading you out of and away from the 'toxic performance art' demanded by the situation makes much more sense! But you also confirm why 'dressing up in words' has always been both dangerous and protective for you. It's as if your mind never rests; it's always hunting down the right figure or trope – and no wonder.

I don't think that we're able to choose our methods as writers, everybody has to use what makes sense to them. I find metaphor endlessly interesting and rewarding. Writing is both safe and dangerous for me, because of my mother's actions. Being visible is agonizing but being invisible, perhaps even more so. I think this is just a more acute version of what everybody goes through. Despite the huge discomfort, it's like walking a tightrope. Fine if you can stay on the line, but the tumbles are inevitable. And even the falls are a sign of success, because I'm practising the art and that's a victory in itself.

Absolutely. Here's to that landing mat, Gwyneth. Iechyd da, a diolch yn fawr iawn.

Jenny Bornholdt

POEMS

Luck

Luckily
the wolf is inside
when the bird
comes to splash about
in what has become
a birdbath.

'Peter and the Wolf'
was childhood.
A bird, a boy,
a wolf. Somewhere
from deep in the forest
the horns sounded
warning.

Just like the song,
the kookaburra sits
in the old oak tree.
Each morning begins
with its long, wild
laugh.

Mountain

Climbers go out in the dark
with head torches and rope.
Sometimes the snow is thigh-
deep. They climb to the death
zone, where it happens, sometimes
in someone's arms, but mostly
alone and cold.

There was a childhood friend,
a climber, I looked after
for a time. Cancer came
and his fine, bony face was cut
and re-made. I'd pick him up
from hospital, alarmingly
unbandaged, and waitresses would gasp
as we ordered. He talked about sleeping
bound to sheer rock, brewing coffee
in the clouds.

Since then, silence.
Like at high altitude
on a clear day – nothing,
they say, but you
and the mountain.

This is not at all
a love story, but still
there's hurt
and fear of loss.

What was the mountain?
Where was hope?
When the avalanche?
Where the rope?

First Aid

Remembering thirty
and two, we resuscitate
a plastic baby, then
an adult. Where's bleeding
gone? Down by bandages
and wounds. Lunch
in the sun and wind.
Trees thrash,
the sea's meringue scuds
up the beach.

When my sister
crashed her motorbike
they cut her clothes off
and handed me a bag
full of feathers.

Home by bus
next to a man
with a fruit
crumble. *Move forward*
said the driver. *Don't
stand in front of that mirror
or we'll all be in
deadly peril.*

Horse

i.m. Jane Maxey

There was talk
of childhood, a horse
named Bucket.

The celebrant said
Please be standing.

An antique black car
took her away – numberplate
h r s e – being hearse or hearsay
horse, even.

Plum

Why wear socks
when your days
are numbered.

Like plums falling
from the tree, frequent
as minutes.

Doing things

Do one thing
and another thing
at the same time.

Do a jigsaw
without looking at the picture
on the lid
of the box.

Name your suitcase
though no trip
is planned. Call it
The Windsor Greys
even though there is only
one of it.

The Greys, you thought,
were Javelin, Atlas, Falkland,
Jupiter. But you misheard entirely –
probably thinking one thing
while doing
another.

Major Apollo was the drum
horse, stepping calm and regular
as heartbeat. Yours
or that of one band member, who,
before going on stage, says
to another
*Don't worry,
just do that thing
that you do.*

I'm about to die.
I can give you the invisibility potion.
Isaac, look out behind...
I was fighting for ages and you were no help.
I'm being chased by, like, 20 guys.
I'm pretty sure there are some teleporting commands.
Oh, I just fell off a roof and broke my leg.
I've got a machete.
Do you need a handsaw?
What's up there?
It's almost night time – I'm on 76 percent.
Do you have any water?
I'm fully dead.

Fires Were Started: Tallinn, March 1944

IAN THOMSON

'Moscow announced this morning that Soviet planes had made a heavy raid on German military trains in the railway centre and port of Tallinn.'

Manchester Guardian, 14 March 1944.

Early in the evening of 9 March 1944, the Soviets began to bomb Estonia's capital, Tallinn. The skyline turned dark; clouds of cinders, lit red by the blaze, floated down over churches, medieval towers, stone-flagged streets. The mile-high roar of magnesium incendiary flames created a firestorm in which 600–700 civilians died (the final count is uncertain), some 20,000 were made homeless and over 600 left wounded. Tallinn had been bombed a total of sixteen times by the Soviets between 1942 and 1943, and more attacks were expected – but not one of this magnitude.

Life as Tallinners had known it came to an end that March night. In a matter of hours, residential districts, hotels, cinemas, factories, hospitals and warehouses were obliterated. The medieval church of St Nicholas was reduced to a hacked-out shell billowing smoke, the synagogue on Maakri Street turned to rubble. In this, the third and final year of the Nazi German occupation, few Tallinners could endure more blackout, bombs and sirens; those who could, left – on lorries, on foot, on over-crowded trains. Among them was my mother, who would not see her hometown again for over half a century.

Today, the unsuspecting tourist can have little idea how close Tallinn came to destruction. At the war's end, St Nicholas was reconstructed with the help of Soviet Estonian and other specialist architects, with each cornice and bit of moulding put back exactly as it had been.

Faced with a bombed city and an acute housing shortage, Estonia's postwar Soviet government put up tenement blocks on the periphery, but in the Old Town they concealed all evidence of the destruction. Baroque buildings were faithfully restored, with squares and green spaces opened up over the shattered streets. Any mention of the attack was discouraged by the censors, who did not welcome accounts of the carnage they had caused. The bombardment was blamed on unspecified 'enemy forces', though anyone who had lived through it knew the truth, and would pass it on to future generations. The efficacy with which Soviet censorship was imposed was anathema to my mother. The memory of that March night remained with her all her life and became her overriding memory of the Hitler–Stalin conflict. In her London exile as an old woman afflicted by dementia she relived the bombardment each Guy Fawkes Night, when buildings and people seemed to be lit up anew by detonations. 'I thought my end had come. I thought I was going to die'.

*

At about 5.40pm the sun went down in a pale glow. There was a grandeur to that sunset which turned the onion domes of Alexander Nevsky Cathedral a gold-pink. Nothing about the evening suggested imminent cataclysm. Trams clanged up and down Adolf Hitler Strasse

(Narva Boulevard). It was snowing lightly and flakes fell on the waters of Tallinn harbour and the Gulf of Finland beyond. In cinemas the matinée show had just ended: *Der unmögliche Herr Pitt* (*The Impossible Mr Pitt)*, a German adventure-thriller, was on at the Kungla; over at the Mars, *Magda*, starring the Swedish-born diva Zarah Leander, was a box office hit[1]. Both cinemas would soon be destroyed. Outside the Central Bus Station – the site of today's Viru Hotel – a policeman in German-issue waterproofs was directing traffic. It was a full moon and everyone agreed that it was a beautiful evening: a moon so bright was unusual for that time of year in the Baltic.

At the Art Hall Café in Freiheitsplatz (Freedom Square) waiters threaded their way across the polished floors taking orders for late tea. They carried trays poised high in the air; others trundled chromium trolleys with glass shelves, on which little Baltic cream curd and marzipan confections were piled. A table of Wehrmacht officers was waiting to be served cups of chicory-substitute coffee; sitting next to the plate-glass windows covered with blackout blinds they might have felt apprehensive. To the south and north of Tallinn, in homes and factories and cinemas, destruction was only minutes away.

At 6.20pm the first air-raid siren wailed. Anti-aircraft guns opened up with a spit of tracers, sending ribbons into the sky. Low-altitude Soviet pathfinder planes dropped green and red marker 'Christmas tree' flares to indicate the targets. The flares cast a bright light as they swayed down by tiny parachute. The play of twinkling reds and greens against the evening sky was beautiful in its way. On the streets below, Tallinners who had not stayed indoors for blackout looked up in wonder as the stars disappeared and the flares began to blaze. The Russian flares made the whole city visible in the dark. 'Birds began to sing at the unexpected arrival of daylight', recalled one witness.[2] On that March night the ancient Hanseatic city was lit up by a great chemical light of Russian flares. The unnatural light shone on posters advertising the latest classical concert, on curtained windows, on hundreds of garden benches and shop windows. Some people were so impressed by the light show that was unfolding that they stood stock still to watch it. Searchlight beams meanwhile raked across the sky, while the flak shells flashed between the beams, and tracer bullets slashed through the darkness. Above it all, the Russian coloured marker flares continued to drift down, spreading a pale light. For all the beauty of the light show, Tallinn was exposed to lethal assault.

The hum of the aero-engines grew more distinct. Having breached the German flak defenses to the east of Tallinn at Lake Ülemiste the estimated 240 bomber planes – Ilyushin 11-4s – flew in high to unleash their bomb blasts and incendiary chemical devices. They came in waves at fifteen-minute and half-hourly intervals. Eye witnesses said they heard a 'shuddering' like an express train before Tallinn was consumed by a smoke so dark that it seemed to force the pace of night. Tallinners took to the boiler rooms, cellars and stairwells of their apartment buildings. They had not been provided with adequate public shelters or bunkers; the German-only bunkers (still visible today) were situated in the cellars of the Wehrmacht high command in Tallinn's Kalamaja district.

In the Art Hall Café customers pushed their way in a panic to the safety of the basement. It was a hundred steps down and people cursed and fell in the crush of bodies. In the darkness there, amid buckets of sand and first-aid equipment, the detonations were getting closer. The crunch of bombs in the streets above was amplified in a maelstrom of dust and tumbling masonry.

Through it all, the moon was a steady spotlight over Tallinn, treacherously lighting up the targets. Bomb bursts in the railway marshalling yard shook Town Hall Square. By 7.15pm there were no longer enough stretcher parties at the Deaconess Hospital on Pärnu Road where Estonian nurses in German uniform were putting up blood transfusions and saline drips. Morphia was in short supply in the wards crowded with casualties and harried-looking doctors. The clove sweetness of anaesthetic and pungency of dried blood thickened as the death toll mounted through the night.

The first attack lasted almost three hours, until 11pm. A rumour circulated that it had been carried out by the pro-Stalin British with their own warplanes and that Soviet women pilots were involved. It was not uncommon for Russian women to take on men's roles in the USSR at this late stage of the war ('Girls – drive a tractor!'). The millions of Red Army casualties in combat meant that Russian women increasingly served in the Soviet armed forces. Some 800,000 of the women were active at the front during the war, many of them operating as snipers. All-female night bomber squadrons were often celebrated on the front page of Russian newspapers for their self-sacrifice and patriotism. The day before Tallinn was bombed, International Women's Day had been celebrated in Leningrad, from where the bombers of Soviet Air Force Regiment 404 took off. If Tallinn was bombed by women with their heads full of Women's Day flower-giving and lavish eating, Estonians should not have been surprised. Soviet Female Aviation Regiments took part later in bomber sorties against Riga, Memel, Libau (Liepaja) and elsewhere in the Baltic. The Germans of course were horrified by the idea of Russian female 'Night Witches' who flew like 'terrorist' banshees in the blacked-out nights of war. Woman power? Impossible. Women should not pilot bomber planes: it affected their morality.

The Golden Lion Hotel at 40 Harju Street where Arthur Ransom, H.G. Wells and Graham Greene had put up in the 1920s and 1930s took a direct hit. So did the neo-classical Estonia Theatre and the Concert Hall building, where the Estonian composer Eduard Tubin's 1944 ballet *Kratt* ('The Goblin') was in its second act. A wall caved in with a sound like cracking plates and the concertgoers hurried down into the levels below ground. All this while the moon continued to gleam over Tallinn steely

1 *Eesti Sõna* ('*The Word of Estonia*') newspaper cinema listings, 9 March 1944.
2 Interview with Mark Sinisoo by Ian Thomson, 30 April 2010.

and bright – a bomber's full moon. The St Petersburg-born dancer Boris Blinov, still costumed in the red cape and green makeup of the Estonian folklore goblin Kratt, ran out of the burning theatre into the snow. Kratt is reputed to appear only during a full moon; now there Kratt was under a full moon, a Dostoevskian horned devil creature in the shape of Blinov. A total of 30,000 costumes in the theatre's storage were burned to cinders, along with fourteen Leipzig-manufacture concert grand pianos[3]. On the building's second floor the sound archive of Estonian Radio Broadcasting was incinerated because German gendarmes prevented anyone from entering: in this way, precious pre-war recordings and technical equipment were lost for good.

This was, by far, the worst recorded night of the war in Tallinn.

The Russian aim was to 'demoralize' and 'terrify' the city's 133,000 inhabitants rather than destroy facilities that would be needed once Hitler was defeated. And there was little doubt now that Hitler would be defeated. After the siege of Leningrad the Russians, in vengeful mood, redoubled their attack on Baltic lands and on Estonia as the gateway to territories in north-west Europe. On 6 March, three days before the Tallinn attack, a four-hour Soviet aerial bombardment had devastated Narva in eastern Estonia. All that was left of that beautiful Baroque city was the castle and the Town Hall. Now it was Tallinn's turn. Flames driven by the wind roared tall as houses on Harju Street, where the cafés Feischner and Eden, the Amor cinema and Astoria restaurant were instantly destroyed. In the Amor alone 150 people died while watching the romantic German comedy *Immer nur Du* (You, Only You), which had introduced a touch of swing with its Fred Astaire-style style dance routines and the hit song 'Darling, What Will Become of the Two of Us?'[4] The fire set light to the cinema's celluloid stock which blazed the night long. A woman had been walking along Harju Street when she hurried into the foyer of the Amor where people were standing packed together. A German soldier outside, waving his arms in warning, shouted: 'You can't stay in there. Get out! Run!' The woman followed the soldier to safety seconds before the Amor took a direct hit and everyone in the foyer died.

The Estonian press reported that twenty-one Soviet aircraft were brought down by Luftwaffe and by Finnish night fighters, crashing in Viru county east of Tallinn. The captured pilots (none of whom, incidentally, was a woman) were probably shot. The bombing continued unabated over Lasnamäe suburb, Kadriorg Park and the Old Town. The Lorup glass factory in Kopli district was ablaze. Behind the factory's every window on every floor a wall of flame was blowing as boxes of fancy glass artefacts melted. Flak splinters whirred through the night as the feasting fire spread to the harbour and beyond. Tallinners wondered if they would survive another moment of this. On Paldiski Road the Capri pasta factory was collapsing amid sulphur-coloured smoke. Tongues of flame leapt round switchbacks in the railway yards on the far side of Toompuiestee Street, where freight trains laden with German military equipment were alive with sparks and then blew up. The city's telephone network and the central exchange had been knocked out, along with the central water system: Tallinn was cut off from the world outside.

In the night sky the dim silvery shapes of the Ilyushin bombers flashed in and out of the spiderweb of white beams streaking up from the anti-aircraft batteries at Lasnamäe. In Battery Jail the Soviet Russian prisoners, many of them Komsomol youth league members, cheered as the bombs fell. 'Our people are coming! Death to the *Germanskis!*' For this insolence they were taken away the next day by the SS and executed. From her office in the prison pharmacy Erika Schein watched in disbelief as the vans arrived in the prison courtyard. 'I saw Komsomol girls being loaded onto those vans in the evening. Van after van. I never saw the girls again. The Germans killed them all.' The fiery glow where the harbour's oil supplies had been hit near the Battery was visible from Helsinki fifty miles away.

A bomb had set fire to the state City Archives and its repository in the Old Town on Rüütli Street. Epp Siimo, the assistant archivist, started in fright from her apartment window at 6 Rüütli Street and decided to salvage what she could. Her path to the repository at 1 Rüütli Street was blocked by a giant gilded weathercock which had come crashing down from the burning Swedish church. Her eyes smarting, Siimo approached the repository in the intensifying heat. From the building's third floor, amid the fume-laden yellow air, she managed to rescue and carry downstairs boxfuls of photographs and newspaper collections. Much of the archive – guild records, Lutheran parish registers – had been microfilmed by German scholars following Hitler's 'repatriation' of Baltic Germans to Reich territories and shipped out to the Centre for the Study of Baltic German Culture in Posen in occupied Poland. Nevertheless, a priceless collection of eighteenth-century Baltic German newspapers and Estonian military records from the interwar period was damaged beyond restoration.

A detonation whipped Siimo in the face; St Nicholas Church at the far end of the street had been hit: the spire burned like a candle and the flames sent hot air gusting down the street at gale-force pressure. The red-hot of the burning spire seared Siimo's hands. Sparks like little red flies settled on her clothes; with the little strength left to her she fought to save and rescue what she could. Sheaves of administrative paperwork were sucked out of the repository into the night: the air was absolutely seething. Siimo, her face soot-blackened and clothes smouldering, waited for the church spire to collapse.

3 *Tallinn tules: Dokumente ja materjale Tallinna pommitamisest 9./10. märtsil 1944,* pps 181-184 (Tallinn on Fire: Documents and Materials Relative to the Bombing of Tallinn, 9/10 March 1944), Tallinna Linnaarhiiv, Tallinn 1997, compiled and edited by Jüri Kivimäe and Lea Kõiv.

4 *Eesti Sõna ('The Word of Estonia')* newspaper cinema listings, 9 March 1944

She was about to turn back when down Rüütli Street came an Estonian police battalion. She urged them to barricade the repository windows against the flames, which they did by fitting metal sheets grabbed from a hardware store; valuable manuscripts were thus saved.[5] Early the next morning a twenty-man voluntary fire unit from the Upper Town (Toompea) sought in vain to find a working fire hydrant: the city water mains were damaged. Still they managed to retrieve fifteenth- and sixteenth-century Lübeck judicial papers, autograph letters by Martin Luther, by Swedish and Danish kings, German and Russian Emperors, papal indulgencies and medieval commercial treaties. Siimo had somehow got beyond fear and was on hand throughout the salvage operation; for her 'noteworthy courage' the German authorities later awarded her 200 Reichsmark (about £400 in today's terms), which she chose to donate to a children's charity.[6] The house where she lived on Rüütli Street had burned to the ground.

My mother was sheltering in the cellar at 71 Tartu Boulevard with her parents and sister. All around the Boulevard, to north, south, east and west, the sky was burning red, with the black branches of the trees visible against the fiery glow. Down in the darkness of the cellar my mother, her parents and her sister heard the detonations and the whistling of bombs overhead. The danger was very close. They had a couple of suitcases containing gas masks, a change of clothes, passports and other documents. The cellar shook and my mother held her nerve as a hail of shrapnel hit the back garden. Splinters made an eerie whistling noise close to the cellar entrance. The bedroom windows upstairs were rattling and the explosions of the guns created lighting effects. Much of the noise and light came from the searchlight units, from the barrage balloons, as well from the squadrons of fighters, and the flak artillery over at Lasnamäe. The flak barrage was a majestic spectacle as Tallinners found their city illuminated by its intensity.

The cellar's one electric light flickered from the concussions above ground as dust sifted down. Two houses away, at number 75, Elmar Ermann died from shrapnel wounds, aged thirty-seven.[7] A third of Tartu Boulevard had now disappeared and still the fires raged.

By 9.15pm the raid seemed to have died away and the German ack-ack guns fell silent. Puffs of flak-burst hung in the air; while a lull of four hours ensued. As the moon hurried behind scattered clouds, Tallinners emerged shaken from their shelters and basements. In twos and threes they hastened through the deserted streets. Across Kreutzwald Street lay six German army horses whose stable had been hit. One horse was alive; in its eyes were reflected the flames of the burning buildings and the billowing smoke and the ruins. The destruction was inexpressible; burning roofs and gables, burning rafters and burning advertising hoardings, and now these horses bleeding and blackened where a bomb had flung them.

My mother's house had survived. Overhead on Tartu Boulevard she watched the last of the Red Air Force bombers depart for Leningrad through gaps in the smoke-clouds: on – on – and then they were out of sight. All was silence again. Tartu Boulevard was left acrid with a smell of burning and sour debris. The heat prickled the skin. The Massoprodukt furniture factory at number 73 was 'burning completely out', my mother recalled.[8] From a distance she watched as the roof caved in amid sparks and secondary detonations of gas and fuel. Andres Rohel (born in Tallinn under Tsar Alexander II in 1860) was burned alive in his house at number 74 opposite: the factory's chimney had toppled onto the roof and burst it apart.[9] Nothing could be more dreadful than this city my mother loved so being devoured by fire. Her father Erich, wasting no time, moved chairs and tableware out into the garden away from the furniture factory's fire next door. He was helped by his neighbour the Orthodox priest Alexander Jürisson, who had been celebrating his thirty-first birthday. 'We had lots of relatives round and aunt Olga had bought us a cake', recalled his wife Larissa. 'We went upstairs and one of us said "Oh my God! Look at the sky!" The bombs were falling and suddenly – boom! – the windows shattered.' In the greenish moonlit sky under the still falling snow my grandfather and the Orthodox priest appeared as ghostly silhouettes; Jürisson in his episcopal coat, my grandfather in his trilby and gaberdine. Orange-red flames from the burning factory were reflected off the walnut polish of the dining table and chairs dragged outside. Aunt Olga was killed when her house was hit in another part of Tallinn.

A thirteen-year-old schoolgirl, Mia Raid, ventured out of her mother's house on Sõja Street (today part of Salme Street) at about 10.15pm, two hours after the first all-clear. She saw flames all round and a kind of tent in the sky made from the white beams of searchlights. 'The smell of the smoke shrouded the street for two weeks afterwards, sharp and acrid', Mia remembered. Round the Baltic Railway Station the nineteenth-century wood-frame houses had been felled whole and left in splinters; no one could rebuild them now. Somehow a train pulled in and passengers were seen to hurry down the platform. Mia watched as one of them drew nearer towards her across the station square. Was it luck that brought her father back to Tallinn on this night of all nights? Boris Raid, an Estonian army officer, had disappeared into the Gulag some time in the summer of 1941; there had been no word of him since. Mia ran forward and propelled herself into her father's arms. 'Having resigned myself to my father's death, his return that night was all the

5 *Tallinn tules*, ibid., pp. 101–4.

6 *Eesti Päevaleht* (Estonian Daily), 1 April 2004, p. 5, 'Tallinn's First Woman Archivist' obituary of Epp Siimo.

7 *Tallinn tules*, ibid., p 220.

8 Interview with Ingrid Thomson by Ian Thomson, 20 June 2011.

9 *Tallinn tules*, ibid., p. 230.

more remarkable', she said.[10] Through the thunder of houses falling apart was this exultant homecoming.

Some Tallinners took advantage of the all-clear to flee. Magda Järve had been sheltering in a farmhouse on the shores of a lake outside Tallinn when her friend Benita woke her up to say that they had to leave. 'We didn't have any exit papers – we just took a chance and went by horse and cart to Tallinn in the hope of catching a train away from the horror.' All they wanted was to go west. 'The further west we got, the safer we would feel, the further from the east', Magda recalled. All round them in the midnight dark lay the dead and wounded by the roadside. 'We didn't stop – it was every man for himself', said Magda. By a fluke the train on which Mia's father had arrived was about to leave for Riga. Magda and her friend got on. 'Benita must have been a better Christian than me, because she could forgive the Russians for what they'd done: I could not.' In Riga they found a city untouched by war. Eventually, by way of Harwich, Magda made her way to London.

At 10.30pm, Lydia Tomson, twenty, emerged from the Art Hall Café cellar to find that nothing moved any more on Freedom Square. 'I had a strange feeling. Everything seemed very quiet but there was this great glow. Tallinn was burning!'[11] She could hear the roar of the conflagration and see the fire a half mile ahead like a black-and-red curtain dropped from the night sky. On Endla Street nearby outside a nursery school a woman lay burning on the pavement like a torch. Lydia walked quickly past her in the direction of her mother's house on Koidu Street. At Tõnismägi on the way there the flames were scything round the bandstand. In the distance on Pärnu Road the bombed-out A.M. Luther plywood factory was lit up 'like a birthday party', Lydia recalled. An eerie solemnity pervaded this part of Tallinn. Lydia picked her way through the malignant landscape where flames threatened to detonate the German ammunition dumps.

When Lydia got to Koidu Street she saw that people had gathered outside number 110, where her mother Antonie lived. The house was a smouldering heap but the people had dragged out furniture and other belongings away from the flames. 'Excuse me miss', a man approached Lydia, 'I think that's your brother over there'.[12] It was not Lydia's brother but her mother, who lay burned where flames had raced up her legs and face. All her hair had gone but she was still just conscious, with one arm protruding. Lydia recalled that she reached out to touch the arm and that it was warm. With the help of bystanders she lifted Antonie out from under the rubble and charred timber and placed her in a blanket-stretcher. On the stretcher Antonie was transported to the Deaconess Hospital not far away. The doctor there indicated that it was useless to try intravenous plasma or blood transfusions – Antonie's breathing was heavy and came in fits – and so he ministered morphine as a

mercy shot. 'It's best for your mother to go now', he said. She was fifty. Lydia and her brother Harry had no sooner made to leave the hospital than the doctor called them back because their mother still had on her wedding ring. 'I wear the ring to this day', Lydia said, indicating the gold band.[13]

Some time after 1am came the second aerial attack. Though less ferocious than the first, it was still purposefully cruel. The anti-aircraft batteries in Lasnamäe began sputtering again and a minute later the sirens wailed. Standing again in Tartu Boulevard my mother watched the flares sail down once more like Christmas spangles when suddenly there was a huge detonation. My mother scarcely had time to hurry back down into the cellar of 71 Tartu Boulevard when the house windows showered down onto the street. A 'second sunset' of orange and rose had spread over Tallinn as the burning city sustained this further wave of bombing. From the cellar my mother heard all over again the piercing howl of falling bombs. The shock wave from one high-explosive bomb knocked her to the ground.

The Russian bomber planes' engine drone was a torment that stayed with some Tallinners all their lives. The attack lasted until a couple of hours before dawn on 10 March. Searchlight beams again reached up through the snow to the returning 60-70 Ilyushin bombers. In the depths of a basement off Luise Street Lydia and her brother Harry Tomson dared not breathe. An ambulance screamed by in the crackling heat as the noise and fires multiplied. From the rubble a brown smoke blew up against the little that was visible of the Tallinn moon.

The all clear ('Raiders Passed') came at about 3am. The second attack had ended. When day broke it was seen that bombs had ploughed up the streets like a field and that much of Tallinn was no longer habitable. The firemen's worst task was opening up cellars still hot and glowing with pockets of carbon monoxide. Bodies were reduced to 'less than half their size – doll-like', recalled a *Lendsalk* (Flying Squad) fire captain.[14] The destruction was so great in some areas that the clean-up brigades had difficulty getting to the houses. The city's central water system had been destroyed and this put the fire brigade's water pumping stations out of action. A key firefighting resource was thus unavailable: Quantities of sand helped to damp down smaller fires but still the flames roared voraciously. It took the firemen five days to bring the fires fully under control; for those five days they hardly slept or ate.

Lydia and Harry abandoned their shelter on Luise Street and made their way to Nõmme four miles away, where they planned to pay a joiner to make a coffin for their mother. The coffin, with every joint and seam bevelled just so, took no time at all to make. Lydia's sister Elfriede ('Fritz') hurried to Tallinn from her home in Haapsalu. Reunited with Lydia and Harry, Elfriede

10 Interview with Mia Foster Raid by Ian Thomson, 15 October 2009.
11 Unpublished memoir by Lydia Tomson Järvik, 'Bombing of Tallinn 9th March 1944' (2012).
12 Interview with Lydia Tomson Järvik by Ian Thomson, 21 March 2012
13 Ibid.
14 Unpublished memoir by Viktor Metsar (undated)

helped to drag the empty coffin through snowfall to Deaconess Hospital where their mother Antonie lay unclaimed in the chapel-mortuary. 'Can you imagine what it was like to pull a parent's coffin six miles through the snow?', Lydia asked me. 'I can tell you the story of how the coffin went on that sledge to the hospital – but the story is only words and this was a matter of personal sorrow, of life and death.'[15] At the hospital Antonie's children had to step over piled-up bodies to reach their mother. Lydia ritually washed the body and enfolded it in a sheet. Elfriede asked three Estonian soldiers on duty outside if they would help to lift the body into the coffin. They obliged and afterwards they very correctly stood to attention and saluted. The coffin was transported by German army van back to Nõmme for burial. A lay preacher in Nõmme – the very joiner who had made the coffin – conducted the service. Spades slipped on the frozen ground at the grave's edge in Sand Cemetery (Liiva kalmistu). Lydia cried without tears. 'It was as if the ducts were frozen', she recalled. The three siblings now had nothing – no parents, no home, no food, no money.

Aili Tatter, a hospital nurse, had been chatting to her volleyball teammates in a gym off Adolf Hitler Strasse when the Hotel Rooma (Rome) at number 30 next door exploded in a shower of sparks. She ran across the road to the basement of the house opposite, where she pulled on her nurse's uniform. Early the next morning she set out on foot for Deaconess Hospital where she was secretary to the German army *Hauptarzt* (main doctor). Everywhere the stench of burned buildings, compact of charred bodies and blackened masonry, dust and pitch, overwhelmed Tatter. She pressed her fox fur against her face. Public transport was at a standstill and the glass in some tramcars had melted. A lorry pulled up beside Tatter and she put her hand up for a lift. The lorry drove with her along what was left of Adolf Hitler Strasse. Smoke rose where columns of earth had spewed up over the treetops. Through the smoke Tatter saw men sweeping up glass outside the Estonian Art Museum, whose collection of Nazi-German racial kitsch artefacts had caught fire. A building on Pärnu Road smouldered into the new day.

The lorry let Tatter down at the hospital, where the wounded were being evacuated by ship across the Gulf of Finland to Danzig (Gdansk) in West Prussia. She had no sooner arrived than she had to bury a nurse colleague called Laurela, who was found in the hospital grounds mutilated beyond recognition by shrapnel. Two weeks later Laurela turned up, carrying as a macabre joke the cross under which Tatter had buried her. Having been written off as dead, Laurela had had gone to Danzig on a German Red Cross ship. 'Even in the midst of this hell there was some comedy', Tatter said.[16]

On Tartu Boulevard, meanwhile, there was still a dusting of snow and, again, no noise. Corpses lay fire-blackened by the roadside and bluish phosphorous flames flickered round them. In the destruction's aftermath relatives searched for their loved ones and tried to find some meaning in their deaths. My mother and her parents and sister were alive at least but they could not possibly stay in the shattered city. In one blasted room on Tartu Boulevard the pictures hung askew and half a staircase lead nowhere. Other buildings resembled dolls' houses, with rooms exposed in cross-section. In these ex-dwellings Tallinners had been born, had lived and loved, and now had died. Only the facades of some buildings survived, and these were hung over with the odour of brick dust and mortality. From the top floor of number 113 a body was being lowered in a wooden box as the Fire Brigade presented arms. It was Maria Peterson, aged eighty-one.[17]

The sun rose on the smoking ruins. In a daze my mother walked down Tartu Boulevard towards the Old Town. A bomb had fallen right on the Plaza-Modern theatre-cinema at number 4, where the German movie *Liebelei und Liebe* (Love and Love) had thrilled Tallinners with its saga of marital betrayal.[18] The combination safe where the owner Ksenia Malahoff Tensing (of Tallinn's renowned Brothers Malahoff fish company) kept her daily cinema takings had melted and warped in the heat. She and her daughter Inna stared in dismay at the safe. 'What else could we do?', Inna asked me half a century later. 'We couldn't even open it!' Inna was nine at the time. 'It was quite a sight for me to see the dead and dying all along Tartu Boulevard.'[19]

Further down Tartu Boulevard, at number 20, the Salamander shoe factory was a mess of exposed roofbeams and twisted iron. A throng of bombed-out men and women passed my mother on their way to Lake Ülemiste, where they hoped to find potable water. White-faced and bedraggled they said to her: 'There's no use going to the Old Town. You can't carry on there – everything's burning.' My mother felt as if she was in a 'strange country' without maps to help her: she might as well navigate by the stars. She turned back home. Gunnar Reiman, a schoolboy, looked in vain for his grandparents' house on Heeringa (Herring) Street: the area had become a wasteland of ash. At a certain point the street no longer seemed to exist; there was not even a discernible path. Reiman managed to find what remained of the house, situated between the Johansen paper mill and the Vellamo soft drinks factory. He dug in the ashes for the suitcase he knew his grandparents had left in the cellar where they sheltered and had somehow survived. Inside what was left of the suitcase he found a blackened metal lump that had been a silver dinner service, and his late father's pocket watch, a tangle now of steel springs and

15 Interview with Lydia Tomson Järvik by Ian Thomson, 21 March 2012

16 Interview with Aili Tatter Eistrat by Ian Thomson, 5 October 2009.

17 *Tallinn tules*, ibid., p. 229.

18 *Liebelei und Liebe* starred the Hungarian-born actor Paul Hörbiger, later famous as the penicillin racketeer Harry Lime's porter in *The Third Man* film.

19 Letter to Ian Thomson from Inna Tensing Ohandi, 27 January 2010.

cogs in a clump of melted gold. It seemed to Reiman that his childhood had ended that night amid the flames.

At Viru Gate bystanders had gathered to view the night's damage, among them the future Estonian writer and diplomat Mark Sinisoo, who remembered the wavering heat that rose from the wreck of the bus station where the timber deposits had caught fire. ('You could almost believe it was a fire to warm your hands on', he said.) Wood had been used instead of petrol to fire up the gas generators attached to the back of the buses, but what buses could run now? Sinisoo was struck dumb by the destruction. 'It can't happen here, we thought – and it did happen', he said, adding: 'The blood was everywhere, and the smell of the wood burning.'[20]

The stench carried over to Town Hall Square, where the sixteenth-century 'Old Thomas' warrior-knight weathervane had crashed to the ground along with its spire. In St Nicholas church adjacent, Christ had been pulled down from His cross; exquisitely carved oak screens and carved misericords (mercy seats) lay strewn amid chunks of stone gable ornamentation and Baroque door embrasures. People were sobbing and weeping. Jewish prison inmates in their familiar striped suits were soon made to shovel rubble to the roadsides under the eyes of the German SS. At a piano in the middle of the rubble a man was playing 'Homeland Air' by Heino Eller, the composer Arvo Pärt's music teacher, a sour-sweet melody in praise of the Estonian nation.

Most of the bombs unleashed on Tallinn had hit civilian homes and public buildings, with very few military installations damaged. A good half of the victims – some 350 children and the elderly – lay unidentified in the hospital mortuaries until they were buried in a mass grave on the Tallinn outskirts. Three days later, on 12 March, my grandfather attended the funeral of his chemistry colleague Roman-Erich Nutov, whose wife Hilda and mother Anna helped to lift the corpse off the back of the cart. The horse shied. Prayers were said. The day was almost dark because of the heavy cloud cover.

The Soviet news agency TASS reported that 'significant raids' had been made on German military trains and 'enemy ships' in Tallinn harbour. The city had been, to use the Nazi German term, *coventriert* or 'Coventrated', meaning 'destroyed utterly'*, after the bomb attack on Coventry in the UK four years earlier. The damage inflicted on Tallinn was as nothing compared to what the British inflicted on German cities. The strategic attacks by the RAF on Hamburg the previous summer in 1943 have passed into the annals of Allied obloquy. (One witness described how children were seared to the pavement in the firestorm 'like fried eels': an estimated 40,000 civilians were killed.) Tallinn was very badly hit all the same. There were no trams anymore, no cinemas, no world, only a steadily mounting anger. Joseph Goebbels's longed-for 'total war', *totaler Krieg,* where death would

come from the sky without warning on those who 'deserved' it, had now been visited on Tallinn. The Russian attack only strengthened Tallinn's resilience. The lesson of history is that bombing raids, even ones as severe as the RAF's against Hamburg, stir up anger and resentment rather than a wish to capitulate. Thus a slogan daubed onto the walls of smouldering buildings in Tallinn – VENGEANCE WILL RISE FROM THE RUINS! – was adopted by Estonians conscripted into the Waffen SS.[21] Estonian men who had hesitated to join German army now hurried to do so.

One incident stayed with my mother above all others, and that was the destruction of her adored orange and lemon plants, which she had grown from pips on her window sill. The blasts had shattered the window and sent glass and curtain-rods flying against the plants. She wept bitterly over their loss. Her parents told her she ought to be ashamed to cry so when hundreds of people had lost their lives. But in her child's mind – as in any child's mind – a personal trivial detail was more important than a world historical event. The shallowness of her concern for her plants was not so different in kind to that of Franz Kafka, when he noted in his diary for 2 August 1914: 'Germany declared war on Russia – afternoon: swimming lesson' (or, for that matter, Patricia Highsmith, who noted in her diary for 22 June 1941: 'Russia and Germany at war!!! Extremely depressed & tired.') The height of trivia juxtaposed with a worldwide catastrophe – the personal and global separated only by a dash or by multiple exclamation marks – seems to sum up my mother's own naïveté and obliviousness to history.

Fires burned for three days with an unusual intensity. Tallinn had endured over 3,068 bombs, 1,725 of them incendiary, the highest tonnage of incendiaries yet dropped anywhere in the Baltic, almost as many as the Luftwaffe dropped on London in the largest raid of the Blitz in 1941. With the Tartu Boulevard house abandoned to flame and ruin and no schools left to attend, my mother and her family had to leave Tallinn. The evacuation centre at 17 Tatari Street gave out timetable information for trains, coaches and other vehicles. 'Sending Children into the Countryside' became the watchword as canteens across Tallinn ladled out quantities of pea soup, noodles, bread and marmalade. Farmers often did not care to open up their homes to dirty-looking, famished evacuees with their bundles and bags; overcrowding led to petty squabbles, with some hosts refusing to provide bedding or fuel for heating. Over 2,000 evacuees left Tallinn in one day alone. For days no newspaper appeared in the city – everything was at a standstill – but on 15 March *Eesti Sõna* sent out the message: 'Estonian Farmers! Do Your Duty! Provide food!' The farmers cooperated and put horse-drawn carts and foodstuffs at the evacuees' disposal.

Eesti Sõna meanwhile raged against the 'terrorist attacks' (*terrorirünnakud*) perpetrated by the 'Russian

20 Interview with Mark Sinisoo by Ian Thomson, 30 April 2010.

* The coinage found an equivalent in the somewhat awkward British "Berlinated", used to describe Britain's retaliatory bombings of Dresden and Hamburg.

21 *Varemeist tõuseb kättemaks!*

barbarians', who were in thrall to the 'half Jew' Lenin and his 'destruction-loving' disciples. ('Russians are incapable of creating a culture of their own, so they must destroy other people's cultures.') In his 'animal-like destructiveness' Stalin aimed to 'sow confusion and panic among the innocent – but he will fail!', because Estonians with their 'cool-headed Nordic spirit' will never bow down. In an extraordinary editorial, 'Stiff Upper Lip', Estonians were exalted as the 'stubborn' race who carry on regardless. The news that pro-Stalinist women In England had been sending gifts of silk scarves to Soviet pilots prompted *Eesti Sõna* to carry a cartoon of a thuggish-looking Soviet soldier with a noose concealed in one hand. 'Thank you, milady', he says to a caricature Englishwoman, 'we hope to put something round *your* necks one day.'

On the night of 14 March, a Tuesday, my mother and her sister Maret were taken by Wehrmacht truck with other bombed-out city dwellers to a property on the rural outskirts, where they stayed for a week prior to being transferred further south to Oisu. Pathetic streams of evacuees pushed what remained of their property on sledges, on push-carts, with packs of stuff on their backs. The so-called 'Flight from the East' – *Flucht aus dem Osten* – had begun. My mother hoped for better times ahead, but as Tallinn smouldered behind her the feeling was of a world irrecoverably lost. 'We didn't even have time to cry', she recalled. 'Everything – silver, furniture, photographs – everything went up in flames or I suppose it was looted.'[22] Half a century on, she could still remember the Tartu Boulevard telephone number: 31954. Nobody could take it away from her. The last Soviet bombs fell on the Estonian capital on 22 September 1944, by which time the Red Army had advanced unstoppably into the Baltic.

22 Interview with Ingrid Thomson by Ian Thomson, 20 March 2009.

An Excerpt from *Like the Night Inside the Eyes*

DANIEL LIPARA

Translated by Robin Myers

My sister and I scattered the ashes in
Bariloche. We climbed the slope with the
box in a backpack. It rattled like wood and
gravel. There were lakes everywhere. The
mountains beyond. Then the wind came.
Most of them landed in a treetop. Then we
took the ski lift down, ate chocolate.
Sometimes joy and pain arrive together. I
open the Iliad, see poplars and poppies. A
woman shoos a fly as her son sleeps
Someone looks up at the stars. After nine
years of war, glimmers of a life everyone
wants back. This is my dad in the crown of
a pine as the force of the wind bears some
of him out to the lakes and stones.

                           as when the south
      and north winds grapple for a forest in the mountains
      they shake the ash trees and the soft-barked dogwood
      the oaks lurch this way and that
      colliding and breaking their branches
      it's a sound from another world

The spear of Ajax enters through the nipple.
The body comes down like a poplar born on
the banks of a lagoon. A carpenter fells it
and cuts its boughs to make a wheel. The
trunk lies prostrate, drying on the shore. He
came to war unmarried, the young son of
Telamon. His mother, a shepherdess,
birthed him on the riverbank when she
brought the sheep down from the hills. She
named him Simeoisios like the river.
Suddenly he appears and is lost among two
hundred forty dead, but his river name rises
from the mouth. There's effort and delay in
the life he lives with his parents, the
marriage he doesn't have, the bank where
he was born. The poem tries to keep him
there a little longer. It can't. Now the
foaming river is a still pool and his soft,
damp torso a dry trunk. This is the glimmer
and the song of the glimmer. The spear of
Ajax entered through the nipple and exited
the shoulder blade. The darkness caught in
his eyes as he ran.

        as a fish
rises from the sea with a single leap snatched up by wind
it lands in the seaweed's fingers
and vanishes into the waves

                as the gleaming surf
ignites and snuffs in silence
when the water senses wind's arrival dreams of storms
great waves hang soundless
they don't know where to fall
until a wind comes and makes its decision

A voice says now like the wind howling in
the water's ears. The spirits of the cows and
fish, the stubborn mosquito. The horse's
verve, the lion's irreversible leap. Thumos,
breath, heart, vitality. Life condensed in the
chest, a force at the mouth of the stomach.
The space where I feel pleasure, wonder,
where I suffer, or joy lingers for a while.
The voice says now like a gust filling the
lungs. The air that slipped out through my
parents' teeth. Me leaving home like
running in a nightmare, breath calling on
the phone. Falling in love. Dad, drunk,
yanking out cables, dancing like a madman
with my sister and me by the hand. The
furor of soldiers with their heads aflame.

Robin Myers writes: The poems published here are excerpted from *Like the Night Inside the Eyes*, by Argentine poet Daniel Lipara: a hybrid work combining brief, diamantine prose with a sequence of poems fashioned from Homeric similes in the *Iliad*. The prose segments explore seismic shifts in the author's own life: his mother's early death, his turbulent relationship with his father, the decision to leave home as a teenager, his mentorship by the late poet Mirta Rosenberg. For their part, the verse poems are 'excavations' (in the vein of Alice Oswald's *Memorial*, an important influence on Lipara) of different Spanish and English translations of the *Iliad*. Lipara's poems explore the Homeric simile as an alternative temporality, an alternative reality, offering up everyday scenes that halt the epic course of war and grief – and then transfigure them with intimacy and awe. Resulting from this prose/poetry juxtaposition is a mysterious, impressionistic exploration of selfhood and change.

Like the Night Inside the Eyes was published in the original Spanish as *Como la noche adentro de los ojos* (Bajolaluna, 2022). This is the first selection from the book to be published in my English translation. Lipara is also the author of *Otra vida* (Bajolaluna, 2018), which I translated as *Another Life* (Eulalia Books, 2021), a book Emily Wilson described as 'a vivid, evocative account of family, place and memory, through Homeric poetry and myth'.

Two Poems

ROOP MAJUMDAR

Krishna's Conch

krishn a did
what krishna was bid

    krishna
    got to it

before
anyone else could

    put a thumb
    in the blowhole

of the deep-
dwelling

    daitya
    and made him

squeal
the boy

    emerged
    from the
    whale's

unlit
belly

    and rose
    to freedom

trailing
red red bubbles

    and ribbons
    of ambergris

guru dakshina
paid

    krishna got down
    to business

from the dead
whale's

    bones
    he hewed the

eponymous conch:
panchajanya

    whose whorls were
    encrustations

of debts
to itself

    so inhospitable
    was its canal

to cosmic
jabber

    you could hear
    your own life

thump
and gurgle

    krishna lifted
    the conch to his lips

and announced
a war

    then sat back
    in his chariot

may everything
equal

    everything
    else

What Singleness Can Bear

i.m. Sonadadubhai

Yesterday was fever.
Is today's feeling
just bad reception
or a blanket response
to the city's perpetual
flinching? I have a few
minutes to think of you.

Not you as such
but your gifts, which
stood for you:
My First Science Encyclopedia,
the Rémy Martin
(Rang'bhai's *medicine*),
the No. 5 that outlived
a marriage of 48 years
and still sits half-full,
stoppered on a shelf.

The decade you
went quiet
we listened in on conjecture,
just as we do now:

the life you lived
in the open and the life
you kept from us
are spliced
behind your back.
Death brings colour.

Where memory goes
I go. Stone bridge
and stone path
that cleaves
to water –
Gif-sur-Yvette.
Three floors up
the helical staircase
to the flat in which
a new normal
entombed you
to your daylong trysts
with Aditi Mohsin
and the kitchen claggy
with St Nectaire and
Comté sat out.

A life spent
acquiring polish:
*I'm not
in the habit
of taking pride
in my ignorance.*

Into the night, then,
when you insisted
you drive to Amin's,
the dashboard lights
of your second-hand
Toyota confounding
your already-
clouded eyes.
From time to time
we both heard
and felt under
our feet the
hubcaps graze
the kerb.
I felt I should say
something but didn't.

Six Poems

REBECCA WATTS

Buttermere

All day I have sat on the lakebed
looking up at the undersides of clouds.
Here and not here.

The lake says there's nothing
to lose anymore.
The water is extremely clear.

En Route to Great Yarmouth

Can anybody actually hear me?
I'm shouting through the car's back window

while the others stand around in the layby laughing
at my act, which isn't an act at all.

1987

The milk bottles are rattling on the tray.
The paper straws are bobbing in the holes.
I shut my eyes and wish myself away
from Smelly Betty and Unkind Peter.

Waiting for Mary Poppins

Rules and cleanliness
are all we want:
to know where we are,
where *naughty* is.

Security in strictures.
A chance to please.
Order and routine.
Bread and jam at five.

The Great Disappointment

After Mary left, we waited
for another well-dressed lady

with a magic handbag to render it
OK. Several candidates

passed through, arriving by bus or by car, but none
appeared to know to bring the bag; situations

arose in which the items we needed
couldn't be found. Some had a distracted

air, as though they'd lost something
but couldn't remember what, glancing

always slightly to the side of where we
stood. Others checked their phones constantly,

as though they themselves were waiting to be rescued.
One even cried.

This was the great disappointment
of our lives: not the fact of our abandonment

by Mary, but the realisation, in view of the data,
that perhaps we'd only dreamt her.

The Miniaturist

Esme draws a picture
but it's only a whisper –
the pencil barely touches the paper

as she ghost-traces a box with a triangle roof
three First-Aid-crossed windows
and a door with a dot for a handle

and beside that a lollypop tree
and on the opposite side a thin chimney
with a pigtail of smoke.

None of the houses she's lived in
looked anything like this,
and still it's home –

where she must shrink right down
until she's only a speck,
invisible in the corner of the glass.

Traditionalism and Tradition

Mark Sedgwick, *Traditionalism* (Pelican) £25

ADRIAN MAY

People who write about tradition come from all directions, often blind to each other. They also rarely see themselves writing as part of a tradition in the broadest sense, which they obviously are. Tradition, strictly as a word, is fairly neutral, as it only means what is passed to us. T.S. Eliot noted in his essay 'Tradition and the Individual Talent' that if people think of it at all, it is as a negative, with the innocent word often used as a stick to beat anyone who is not immediately anti, and for some kind of obeisance to the non-god of progress. My own favourite remark about the word is in Raymond Williams *Keywords* (1976), which is almost a throwaway at the end of the alphabetical entry: 'the word moves again and again towards' a negative, past-heavy view. 'Considering only what has been handed down to us, and how various it actually is, this, in its own way, is both a betrayal and a surrender.' Williams's still unusually positive view reinforces an earlier point he makes about 'the sense of tradition as active process'.

This sums up my own feeling about the topic, especially in relation to literature and to its related genres, folk and popular song. It also gives an indication of how wide I have cast my net over many years to find useful positive writings on tradition. These are sometimes both small and disparate positives, which are often not even at the centre of anyone's work. Apart from Eliot and Williams, at present a chapter from the political sociologist Anthony Gidden's Reith Lectures, 'Runaway World', and Herbert Read's 'To Hell with Culture' could be added to Bob Dylan, Robert Burns and Ted Hughes, as favourites. Here I have to declare an interest: my book *Tradition in Creative Writing* is the most positive view I could make. It has a design of tree roots on the cover, as does *Traditionalism: The Radical Project for Restoring Sacred Order* by Mark Sedgwick. Yet Sedgwick barely mentions any of the writers on the topic that I do and, to be fair, the reverse is true, too.

I had heard of 'traditionalism' but, like many things mentioned by academics in big books, it seemed dull and only to do with a kind of universalist view of religion. Mark Sedgwick's book is readable and interesting, even challenging, but I still feel that I need to address the gulf between his capitalised 'ism' and my lower-case for creativity. René Guénon, whom Sedgwick cites as the founder of the topic, had the view that everything modern was wrong and that to cure *The Crisis of the Modern World*, as in his book of 1942, we had to return to a religious tradition and restore it, thus averting his titular crisis. To someone raised on an active view of tradition, in folk music for example, as I was, this seemed the outlook of one I might politely call a *purist*, even if I kind of got what he was getting at.

Purists and the 'folk police' are frightening to the living tradition, as they tend to deny the validity of anything you do, and I fear this might be why *Traditionalism* ignores so much that I would call traditional. Even Bob Dylan, in his autobiography, *Chronicles*, records encounters with such forbidding figures, where he is not sure if help is being offered or if they are just putting him down. I suspect the paradoxically traditional influences on 'modernism' might be regarded by purists as fakes, not as evidence of life, as I see them.

Sedgwick's carefully written book even risks itself being seen negatively, which I think is not his intention, given his career devotion to the topic. I first heard of it on Radio 4's *Thinking Allowed* programme (31 January 2024), where the influence on Putin and Trump of writers and thinkers claimed as 'Traditionalist' was highlighted at the expense of any positive message. From the beginning, in a familiarly academic way (a tradition?), the author wants to have it both ways. His subtitle and first sentence speak of the 'radical project for restoring sacred order' before, in the sentence that follows, claiming to be 'professionally neutral' and that his conclusions are 'mixed'. So, for me, the narrowing headline world of 'growth' and 'progress' are not as challenged as I had hoped and there is a feeling that any re-enchantment is distant and marginal, however important or interesting. Not engaging with active tradition, other than the deeply religious, seems a deliberate sidelining of anything usefully alive in the word.

The long philosophical and metaphysical chapter on 'Self-realization' lost me at times, especially when the only recent example Sedgwick offers is Jordan Peterson, whose talent for self-publicity might suggest he belongs among the moderns, rather. Religion in general as mythically neglected is familiar to me and to many writers, while the chapter on nature and tradition seems safe and uncontroversial ground, with some positive and unusual examples.

Whatever else the book does, it has provided me with a reading list, as I am always keen to see anyone thinking about tradition, in any way other than the reductive views of the authors and editors (Eric Hobsbaum et al) of *The Invention of Tradition*. This book is not mentioned either, though it was a very well known in the '80s, when it had seemed to kill the whole subject in academia for decades. Despite some chosen upper-class examples, such as Sir John Tavener and King Charles III, there are other writers, such as Guénon himself and Coomaraswamy, that demand further reading from me.

Next to Guénon's *The Crisis of the Modern World* in Essex University library was a book called *The Past in Ruins*. As it, too, looked old, I pulled it down, peering at the faded black spine. This turned out to be David Gross's 1992 book, subtitled 'Tradition and the Critique of Modernity'. With a mixture of my own guilty incompetence at research and pleasure, I have found this book to be one of the best I have seen on the topic, and one with an intelligent and positive perspective. The fact that the word 'tradition' was not in the actual title of either book might excuse me a bit. But this fascinating study does remind me of how diffuse the bibliography of tradition can be.

None of the reviews of *Traditionalism* I have seen mention what I take to be a big omission. The loss of myth is not new to poetry, literature or the arts generally, and Guénon's main thinkers were not the first to remark on it. To be fair, Guénon does mention John Ruskin. But the cultural influence of figures such as Yeats, T.S. Eliot and other 'modernists' seems too significant to be ignored. Also somehow missing is the paradox that much 'modernism', in art generally and literature particularly, embodied a return to a kind of traditionalism: Stravinsky, Picasso, Joyce and especially the musical move towards rediscovering folk music among European composers at around the same time as Guénon's work. This is all essential to understanding a big part of literary history and influence. The thing Eliot pointed out about needing to know tradition to be contemporary, or simply 'the oldest yet the latest thing', seems absent, even though Tavener is quoted as speaking of the need to be a 'practicing artist' to understand tradition.

Some of his unusual examples are potent, however. The 'feminine community' called Aristasia, founded by an Englishwoman in Ireland, sounds genuinely different and challenging, and offers a defiant, alternative view from the '80s. The book is clearly written, well edited and offering useful summaries, meaning that it speaks of something difficult and sometimes controversial in a decent and well-tempered way.

The convention which *Traditionalism* is part of, though, is one of academic writing of a particular kind, where the 'neutral' stance and the dedication to the 'ism' can seem pasted on to the content after the fact. I think no one called the capitalised Enlightenment by that grand name at the time, for instance, and do not get me started on 'Post-modernism'. But the risk with this kind of work is that of a catch-all type of inclusion and exclusion which looks like balance but comes across as a lack of passionate opinion, with, in the worst cases, a stating of the obvious at its centre. Is this a modern convention, as I suspect, rather than a tradition, writing-wise? A book with advocacy of tradition or Traditionalism might be more refreshing, even more 'restorative'. There is a danger that academics, with their professed neutrality, can seem merely judgmental and disengaged.

The book has me interested but I would like to know what the author really thinks, especially when we get a glimpse of his early interest in Sufism. Having just read a book about J.D. Salinger, with his interest in Vedanta, I wonder if he fits in, with his rejection even of publication; did that make him a Traditionalist? Also, American academic writers on religion often seem braver and more opinionated these days, which is to their benefit.

Myths, traditionally, are very often about their own restoration, so have a traditional agenda, as with Dionysus, the returning god of nature, in Euripides' *The Bacchae*, reminding the corrupt city of its debt to fertility. Or as Jessie L. Weston said in the grail monomyth work *From Ritual to Romance*, 'the task of the hero is that of restoration'. Mark Sedgwick's tale is of the traditional mythic genre of the return of myth to heal the world, even if that sometimes seems missing here.

from Kit Smart's Ark

JUDITH WOOLF

for Neil Corcoran

A is for Anchovy

Let David Attenborough rejoice with the Anchovy –
I beheld and lo! a great multitude!

blindsided by youth
you saw the seas glitter
each fish a silver sliver
enough, you thought, for ever

clear-sighted now in age
you hold a blue planet
like a diminishing bait ball
do not let it fall

D is for Dragon-fly

Let David Hockney bless with the Dragon-fly,
who sails over the pond by the wood-side and feedeth on the cressies.

in recognition of secret knowledge shared
let Dürer's tiny dragonfly take flight
from its bottom right-hand corner
and land lightly on an iPad lily pad
in a finger painting of smaller trees near water

J is for Junco

Let Emily Dickinson rejoice with Junco the Reed Sparrow.

There is a Bird – evades the Sight
She's drest so modestly
But there's a passion – in her Breast –
A Darkness – in her Eye –

And heedless – of a Listening Ear –
She trills – all Summer long –
Who could believe – a Form – so Small –
Holds such a Wealth – of Song –

L is for Lion

Let Derek Jarman come forth with a Lion.
For a LION roars HIMSELF compleat from head to tail.

between the sea and the barren strand
living in borrowed time
you gathered stones together
to make a garden bloom

your breast no longer a bastion
your eye a fading coal
you showed how a man can speak himself
from the crown of his head to his soul

V is for Vulture

Let Maggi Hambling rejoice with the Vultur
who is strength and fierceness.

sitting hunched and brooding
or soaring the thermals
more than eagle eyed

any subject you light on
is stripped to the bone

Z is for Zebra

Let Kit Smart bless with the Zebra,
whose stripes are so clear that no one could paint them better.

Queen Charlotte's ass
a target for ribaldry
but a fitting gift for a princess
with African ancestry
who was yet to discover how hard
her married life would be

let Nannerl greet in the zebra
a fellow prodigy of nature
let George Stubbs paint in the zebra
the solitude of a displaced creature
let Kit Smart bless in the zebra
a poor captive and prisoner

Present Future Imperfect Continuous

JANE HOUSTON

let's say your child is turning 8 and refuses
to tell the time so as a *learning activity*
you make a cake for her to ice with a clock face
and she pipes numbers in slippery trails of pink
squeezing the piping bag hard it is going to burst
and icing will ooze glossy and sticky and you
will not be able control how the hours will merge
to a shiny mass or how your child will cram
melting minutes in her face

come on get off the bus! let's say you're
pushing down the aisle behind the man
you love and on the pavement your child
is flowing out of her grandmother's arms
toward you *we're back we told you we'll
always come back* and let's say you both
in that moment do believe you will forever
hold a shape where she can pour herself
but let's also say that right now your child
is opening the door into this room
where you are writing and she needs
she needs you and let's say you turn to her
smiling instead of what you actually do

you get very old and your child comes to visit
bringing a gift box with an amber necklace
but when you lift it to the light the muddy colour
of the stones distresses her and she has a tantrum
which in turn distresses the other residents
the helpers gather trying to shush everyone
and let's say that during this you just study
how the beads glow until its time for you to reach
for her and she sobs into you and knots her fingers
into yours and her teardrops slow to the pace
of resin oozing from a wounded pine

the clocks have gone forward
evening light falls on the bare sycamores
the rooks are noisy and you see something
out of place on the sofa a small brown
something it is moving it is alive
it has a bat face it is stretching out
a translucent bat wing it is a bat
and what do you do? you get yellow
gloves a bat could bite through
and you wear them to scoop the bat
into your palm and you think about rabies
as you take the bat into your garden and put it
on a log in the woodpile and you return
several times that evening to check on the bat
it is moving very slowly along the log
each time you check it has travelled a little
should you feed it? is it safe from the rooks?

your child's face has been painted
perhaps as a puppy perhaps as a leopard
and she is crying her puppy/leopard spots off
to get away from you and she's running
down the pavement and kicks a pile
of horse shit onto the road and she
is the screaming sand in her throat
is the grass blade in her sock
is the ant in the ant army crawling
over the horse dung and you catch her
in your clutch of rings and nails but she
wriggles away
and you raise your hand above her
and let's say that you let it fall
we agree that you let it fall

let's say your child is weeks old
and you are washing her in a plastic
bath in front of an electric bar heater
not too close! and she is kicking her feet
happily and as the water is cooling
you lift her out the bath and trigger her
startle reflex she throws her limbs out
and inhales deeply and into this silence
hurtles the bathwater and the electricity
and the room and your whole house
and in fact all the houses of your area
so that when her scream comes
all that is left is you holding your naked baby
with the ribs of your town curving
around you empty and bleached

come on get on the bus! this is a different bus
it's a school bus pulling up outside your house
and your child is crossing the road and giggling
she has tucked you into her pocket and is patting
you as she climbs up the steps onto the bus
and patting you again when she takes her seat
and with her other hand she is pressing
her fingertips on the window to print
a wave and a full size version of you
is standing at the bus stop waving back

La Géante

ALEX WONG

from the sonnet of Baudelaire

In the dim forgotten age when Mother Nature,
Brimming with a potent verve,
Was every day conceiving prodigies,

I would have liked
  to pass my days
Close to a giantess,
   still in her youth:
To lie with her, like some voluptuous cat
At the feet of a supine queen.

I should have liked to see her body
      flourish with the soul inside it –
See her getting larger, getting larger,
Growing through her terrible amusements;

To guess, by scrying in the humid fogs
Hovering in her eyes, what sombre fires
Dark in the heart she might be brooding over;

To scan at ease her monumental forms;
To clamber on the ramps of colossal knees; –
And in the summer, when great morbid suns
Induced her in her lassitude to
      spread herself out long over the landscape,

I would doze
  without a care
In the shadows
  of her breasts,
A hamlet all at peace at the foot of a mountain.

from *What Is Poetry?*

PHILIP TERRY

In the late summer of 2023 I received through the post a strange book from the poet Oliver Reynolds entitled *Seven Romes Eight*. It looked handmade, with a small block of marble glued to the cover, paint daubed over a ragged cloth spine, pieces of crushed paper stuck to some of the pages, blue electrical wire taped to some of the others. It was published by Sosban, a publisher I could find no trace of online. Its pages contained various versions of a sonnet I had always thought was the work of Joachim du Bellay – in Latin, French, English, Spanish – on how the once great city of Rome had collapsed into ruins. My interest in versioning was known to Reynolds – he had read my own campus versions of du Bellay published under the title *Bad Times* – but as I read on I quickly saw that this was not just an anthology of different versions of du Bellay, rather it revealed the little-known fact that the French poem was always already a translation, from the Latin of Janus Vitalis of Palermo. For a long time, it seems, the French had assumed the poem was by du Bellay, and a version in Spanish had been written by Quevedo, whose Spanish readers had likewise taken it for an original. Reynolds quotes the following exchange from Boswell's *The Life of Samuel Johnson*:

> CAMBRIDGE: 'A Spanish writer has this thought in a poetical conceit. After observing that most of the solid structures of Rome totally perished, while the Tiber remains the same, he adds: '*La que era Firme huió solamente, / Lo Fugitivo permanence y dura*' ('Only the static disappeared; the fugitive remains and endures.')
> JOHNSON: 'Sir, that is taken from *Janus Vitalis*: '— — — immota labescunt; / Et que perpetuó sunt agitate manent.' ('The motionless disappears; it is constant motion which abides.')

And it goes on, as authors continue to proliferate in a Borgesian dance. Czesław Miłosz sums it all up in *The Witness of Poetry*: 'at the turn of the sixteenth century a Frenchman was able to read a poem on the ruins of Rome signed Joachim du Bellay; a Pole knew the same poem as the work of Mikolaj Sep-Szarzynski; a Spaniard, as the work of Francesco de Quevedo; while the true author, whom the others adopted without scruple, was a little-known humanist, Ianus Vitalis of Palermo.'

In total, the volume contains ten versions of the poem, one in Latin, one in French, one in Spanish, and seven in English. It concludes with a version by Seamus Heaney, published in the *New England Review* of October 2013, one of the last poems Heaney had been working on before his death. Paul Muldoon comments: 'In the face if this terrible loss, we may take comfort in our profound sense that, like the Tiber, Seamus Heaney's work will continue to be a constant in our lives.' According to Muldoon, Heaney, like many of his predecessors, thought he was translating a poem by du Bellay. He was not. I like to think of the shade of Seamus Heaney, that arch recycler and ventriloquist, always alert to poetry's ironies, bumping into some of the other poets gathered in Reynolds remarkable anthology, and finding out for the first time about the poem's disingenuous poetical history. He'd find it all very good craic.

*

Reading Wilfred Owen's *Collected Letters*, their gentle descriptions of small-town life intensify unknowingly as 1914 approaches. This postcard to his mother, who is recovering from an operation where she is 'torn up', with its references to 'the Gas!' and the '5 Army Officers' Owen has been teaching in Bordeaux, sent on 17 September 1913, anticipates in its accidental imagery everything that is to follow, as the ticking of the bicycle in Heaney's 'A Constable Calls' from *North* anticipates the Troubles:

> Mary did indeed tell me you were to be torn up into 10 parts on Saturday: but, reading it on Sunday, I did not gather it was Sat. of last week, but thought it was several days off. Do not think me stony, therefore, that I made no mention of it in the letter; (& I was as unsuspecting on Sat. as you could wish). But it seems marvellous that you can have gone through a ten-times-heated-horror; and worst of all, the Gas! What courage! It shames us all! May you be well cherished & in bed this week! The thought of you in 'the Chair' inspires me to despise my little annoyances. Last night, curiously enough after writing my letter, & getting into bed my legs ached as if they were on the racks. But it was only a playful trick of the Humidity & cold; and did not prevent me from taking a class this aftern. of 5 Army Officers. This was quite interesting, & did me good. I feel confident of keeping on.
>
> Your own, W

*

In Palermo, reading Ariosto in Italian for the first time, it suddenly strikes me that the fundamental difference between Ariosto and Spenser is *speed*. The *story* is always in the foreground in Ariosto, it zips along at an articulated pace, whereas in Spenser the movement is one of elaboration, of stepping sideways, of digging deeper – as in Andrew Hadfield's magisterial exposition of the poem – so that we end up stuck in a bog.

*

'The whole... of... the world... is given over to, commended to, and thus subjected to the command of self-assertive production', writes Heidegger in his essay 'What Are Poets For?' If Heidegger is right, and if he is still right in the era of neoliberalism, then the most radical response open to the poet is to stop writing. We can see traces of this ultimate gesture in all minimalist poetry, in Duchamp's claim, late in his life, to have given up art for chess, and in the single word and single letter poems of François Le Lionnais of the Oulipo. Who the poets of genius were, who stopped writing altogether, perhaps having never begun, we will never know.

*

If, for Rousseau and the Romantics, the child is the father of the man, for Larkin the child is 'fucked up', and childhood is characterised by awkwardness, unhappiness and boredom. In an interview with John Haffenden Larkin says: 'If you're more interesting as a child than as a grown-up, what's the point in growing up? I think grown-ups are nicer than children. I hated everybody when I was a child, or I thought I did. When I grew up, I realized that what I hated was children.' And he goes on: 'Of course, I speak as a childless person: I've never lived in hideous contact with them, having toast flung about at breakfast and so on. Perhaps worse than toast. The whole doctrine of original sin implies that children are awful, don't you think? The nearer you are to being born, the worse you are.' It is here, more than anywhere, that Larkin nails his anti-romantic colours to the mast. They are the colours, in Heaney's words, of 'A nine-to-five man who had seen poetry.'

*

Tucked away in the closing lines of 'A Note on War Poetry' (1942), which had been written at the request of Miss Storm Jameson and which is included in the short section entitled 'Occasional Verses' at the end of his *Collected Poems* (1909–62), Eliot offers the following definition of poetry: what we call 'poetry', he writes (line 24), which 'May be affirmed in verse' (line 25), is 'the abstract conception' (line 22) 'Of private experience at its greatest intensity' (line 23) 'Becoming universal' (line 24). The majority of Eliot's statements on poetry, especially on his own poetry, tend to emphasise impersonality, as in his essay 'Tradition and the Individual Talent', which in some respects anticipates Roland Barthes's 'The Death of the Author'; here, in stark contrast, we see Eliot, while not abandoning the idea that poetry must be 'abstract' and 'universal', placing personal experience – not just any experience, but experience 'at its greatest intensity' – back at the very heart and origin of poetry.

*

An intersectional poem, entitled *Prelude Lost*, consisting of the text of *The Prelude* reduced to the words it shares with *Paradise Lost*. Words that are not common to the two texts are erased.

*

Poetry: philosophy filtered through private minds and lives, entertainment for the pitiful obsessive, anything that can't classify itself, hates you for asking, a darkling thrush, nationalism veiled in art subsidies, proud of fog, attainable enigma, unread ignored inspired, thought without influence, possible wor(l)ds, elitist half manic craft, aconite gaze, beautiful smelling lies.

(Gregory Betts)

*

'The poetry written by most of the "promising" poets of the fifties', says Geoffrey Hill, 'seemed to me to stem from a basic misconception about the nature of poetry and language, and I must say that my views have changed very little since then. It seemed to me that young poets of that time were writing poetry of one or two kinds, neither of which was my kind. They were either Empsonian in the most arid sense, writing cerebral conundrums... or they were narrating amorous adventures and travel anecdotes in language that was the equivalent of painting-by-numbers.' Hill's arid Empsonians, perhaps, are poets like Randall Jarrell and I.A. Richards, a tradition which would later give rise to Martian poetry, and which still has advocates today; his auto-biographical painting-by-numbers poets perhaps include Robert Lowell and Lawrence Durrell, a tradition that lives on (often vibrantly) in the new confessionalism of writers such as Clare Pollard and Selima Hill. If Hill himself represents a third way, as he suggests, then it is perhaps the tradition of high seriousness and high culture that has its roots in the poetry of T.S. Eliot, but curiously, today, it is this tradition which seems the most arid of the three, living on in the Eliotic simulations of Toby Martinez de las Rivas, whose *Floodmeadow* comes complete with Sanskrit and Notes. And yet, much of the most vibrant, exciting and surprising poetry around today has roots in *none* of Hill's categories – rather it responds to the explosions of language and culture that have evolved *since* the fifties, in pop and dub poetry, in visual and sound poetry, in Oulipo and L-A-N-G-U-A-G-E poetry, in spoken word poetry, in instagram poetry, in code poetry and digital poetry, in LGBTQ+ poetry, in talk poetry, in experimental translation, in minimalist poetry and nature poetry, in Feminist poetry, in poem-objects and film poems, in kinetic poetry, in installation poetry, and in concrete poetry and the new concrete.

*

Poetry usually comes between two covers, though it can sometimes appear on walls, as with the mural limericks of Angry Dan, or even on T-shirts, or posters. The work of Stephen Emmerson has yet to appear on walls and T-shirts, as far as I am aware, but while it has appeared between covers, like conventional books of poetry, and has been distributed on at least one poster, it increasingly appears in boxes. The boxes are full of strange drawings and signs to inspire poems, templates with different shaped 'windows' to place over newspapers, novels or magazines to create found poems, or, as with

A Box of Ideas, not poems as such, but *ideas* for poems, or *ideas* for books of poems. The brief texts are printed on white card (15.5 x 10.5 cm) and are full of enigmatic suggestions, such as: 'A book of poems made up of synopses of other books of poems'; 'A book of poems called *Writing not Writing* in which every page contains a description of something that has distracted the writer from writing'; 'A book of poems made entirely out of footnotes'; or, among the longer ones, 'A book of poems in the form of a pharmacological experiment. Ten volunteers are selected and sent a bottle of placebo pills and instructed to take one every day at lunchtime for fourteen days. On the fifteenth day they must then write as many poems as they can over a twenty-four-hour period. The resulting texts should be sent back to the address on the bottle of pills. These texts are then collated and published as a book of poems called *The Experiment*.' The book doesn't come with instructions, but it slyly suggests that the ideas presented in the box could be picked up by the reader and realised as books. Who, or what, *is* the reader here? Does the reader, as she reads the contents of the box, *become* the writer? Does the reader find herself acting as a collaborator? Or is the reader's labour cynically co-opted to perform the work of the writer in absentia, without pay?

*

'The only reality is Beauty and Its only perfect expression is Poetry.' (Mallarmé, *letter to Henri Cazalis, 14 May 1867*)

*

When we think of prose that is 'poetic' we tend to think of the Joyce of *Ulysses* and *Finnegans Wake*, or the late novels of Virginia Woolf, but there is a case to be made for Proust. If, as Robert Frost put it, 'Poetry is what gets lost in translation', then Proust's radical untranslatability would support this view. Proust begins his novel with the deceptively simple words 'Longtemps, je me suis couché de bonne heure'. It looks straightforward to translate, but it isn't as we will see. In the first English translation, by Scott Moncrieff, it is rendered: 'For a long time I used to go to bed early.' That seems logical enough, and it works, but it misses the comma in Proust, which immediately introduces a hesitation, a tentativeness, which is one of the great joys of reading Proust. A much more recent translation, by Lydia Davis, published by Penguin in 2002, begins: 'For a long time, I went to bed early'. That works too – 'went' is a more satisfactory translation than Moncrieff's 'used to go' – and for me it's an improvement in that it restores the important comma in Proust's French, even if it makes the sentence look as though it divides neatly into two parts, whereas the Proust has three – involving time, then going to bed, then timeliness. It also has the same syllable count as the French. It is almost perfect. But it doesn't put an end to the translation of Proust once and for all. For that would be impossible, even with this seemingly straightforward first sentence. One reason it is impossible is that the French continues to unfold as we read the novel, so that the meanings, the connotations, of this first sen-

tence actually change and continue to grow as we read. One very Proustian moment is when the narrator wakes up, and finds that the self is not simply *there* at the moment of waking, but has to be remembered, reconstituted, put together again, on a daily basis. There is no hint of this in 'For a long time, I went to bed early', but there *is* a hint of this in 'Longtemps, je me suis couché de bonne heure.' The sense that the self is wiped clean every day by sleep, and therefore has to be rebuilt in the morning, is hinted at in the *sound* of the French, where behind 'je me suis' it is possible – especially if we imagine a state of sleep or near-sleep – to hear the phrase 'je m'essuie', 'I dry myself', or 'I wipe myself clean'. Similarly, 'de bonne heure', literally 'early', as in the translations of both Scott Moncrieff and Lydia Davis, conceals another word, 'bonheur' (happiness), which conveys something of the pleasure which Marcel takes in this moment of going to bed and going to sleep, particularly the moment when his mother comes up to give him a goodnight kiss. And perhaps this pleasure has a more sexual aspect at times, as hinted at again in the concealed phrase 'je m'essuie' – Marcel goes to bed to *wipe himself* – as he also does, doubly, in the toilet, which later in the same chapter we read is Marcel's favourite place and which (in Davis's translation) 'for a long time served me as a refuge, no doubt because it was the only one I was permitted to lock, for all those occupations of mine that demanded inviolable solitude: reading, reverie, tears and sensual pleasure'. Going to bed, it turns out, often conceals something else, as when Swann tells Marcel's parents that he is going home to bed, then slips off to hang out in high society. Following the same line of thought, in 'longtemps' I hear a hidden 'ton' (tone), which takes us to the sound world, the overheard, of the young Marcel as he lies in bed, sounds and voices drifting upstairs and noises coming in from the garden. Proust's famous sentence about going to bed, literally 'lying down', itself, we come to see, contains layers (couches) made up of meanings that themselves are lying down (couché), but which, like the sleeping Marcel, are ready to awaken at any moment. And so it goes on. As one reads, the complexities continue to unfold, there is displeasure mixed with pleasure, here, as Marcel is separated from his mother, and there are other emotions, other sensations, such as the feeling, sometimes, of being *sent to* bed (away from the company of adults), rather than just *going to* bed, or the feeling of being *taken* to bed, or *taking oneself* to bed (the verb in French is reflexive), and then there are all the scenes throughout this vast novel (or novels) involving bedrooms and beds, which retrospectively cast their shadow back on this primal scene, showing it in ever new colours and lights as in a magic lantern show. This magical strain, evoked early in the novel, reaches its ne plus ultra in *La Prisonnière*, where Marcel is visited in his bedroom by Céleste Albaret. Proust recounts the following exchange between Céleste and Marcel (Carol Clark's translation): 'O heavenly majesty set down on a bed [she exclaims] – Why heavenly, Céleste? – Oh, because you're like nobody else, you're quite wrong if you think you have anything in common with those who tread the humble earth. – Well, why "set down", then? – Because you don't look like a man lying down, you're not *in* bed, it looks as if angels flew down and put you there.' All of a sudden, the mundane act of going to bed takes on an almost magical realist aspect, where the occupant seems to *float* above the covers, evoking the mind of the creative artist, of Marcel, as it floats through the flotsam of his daily life, sculpting it into the forms that will become this vast novel. There is really no way to capture all of this, no way out of the conclusion that Proust is radically *untranslatable*. Yet it is in seeing this *untranslatability* that we see too the poetic in Proust: his meanings, as in a poem by his near contemporary Mallarmé, can never be exhausted, and the more you pore over the text the more you see. The 'cou' in 'couché', for example, makes me think of 'queue' (bottom, tail), which in turn makes me think of Proust's fourth volume, *Sodome et Gomorrhe* (1921–2), as well as the subsequent volumes, *La Prisonnière* (1923) and *Albertine disparue* (1925), and if you combine 'queue' with 'je m'essuie', a possible outlying translation of Proust's opening that begins 'For a long time, I wiped my bottom...' starts to emerge. Astonishing too, an obsolete word in English for a late night reception – might Proust have heard it? – is 'couchee', which hints at another, and astounding, subliminal sense of Proust's opening sentence, equally impossible to translate, that seems to capture, as in a miniature kept in a secret locket, the entire contents of the novel in nine words: 'For a long time, I went to receptions early'.

*

'*Occasional Verse.* The poet laureate of England holds the one public office in the Western world whose main function is to produce occasional verse. It is an old and respected tradition that the official poet should produce a poem in honour of various important occasions, such as the Queen's birthday. Good poetry, unfortunately, is not always produced to order...'

(Frances Stillman)

*

'After all, poetry is a thing depending almost entirely on words. There are Shites, of course, who think it does (first stage fuckers) and spend their time (Maugham!!!) juggling with "richly brocaded" words. These men are shitpans, come-pots and toss-bottles. Then you get the intellectual fuckers (M. Arnold) who say "Poetry is written with ideas." Their obstreperous failures cover pages of literary history. Then, among the greatest poets, you get men whose poetry depends entirely upon words again. *This because*: Poetry depending on ideas must depend on *new* ideas to be any good. *But* no new ideas are any good; all ideas that are any use are as old as the human race – *fundamental* ideas: *therefore*: poetry consists in expressing these old & wellworn ideas & emotions in new and exciting forms so that the emotion or idea emerges new again. All this is quite elementary. But it's rather easy to forget.' (Larkin, *letter to J.B. Sutton, 23 June 1941*.)

*

Hardy at his worst, as in 'At Castle Boterel', sounds like Poe, the strained rhyme as predictable as his idea of Fate:

I look and see it there, shrinking, shrinking,
　　I look back at it amid the rain
For the very last time; for my sand is sinking,
　　And I shall traverse old love's domain
　　　　Never again.

*

Writing machines. Writing machines have a long history. Swift, in *Gulliver's Travels*, describes a machine operated by handles generating sentences which are then gathered together to 'give the World a complete Body of all Arts and Sciences', and more recently Oulipo have created their own writing machines where a text has all its nouns changed by moving on seven places in a dictionary: 'To be or not to be that is the quiche'. Today, AI technologies give access to a new breed of writing machines, underpinned by algorithms and code, that generate text instantly. You can ask for a song, or a story in the style of Virginia Woolf, and it's there in seconds. The song will have a conventional verse-chorus structure, and the story will lack Woolf's finesse, but these things will come. Artists and poets have already been working with AI to generate metamorphic art, and experimental novelists such as Tom Jenks have used DeepAI to create illustrations, but the future for writing more generally we can only imagine. My guess is that AI will affect different types of writing in different ways: more generic writing, where there's a fixed plot and characters, as in Dumas's collaboratively written *The Three Musketeers*, will be easy to reproduce by machine, and so will some types of science-fiction and romance as well as greeting card verse. Writers of Mills and Boon and verse of this kind will soon be out of a job. But more esoteric masterpieces are less likely to be threatened. It's hard to see AI producing *Ulysses*, or *The Waste Land*.

While the rest of us worry about the future of writing in the age of AI, the poet Peter McCarey has been busy creating his own breed of writing machines, more like the imaginary creations of William Heath Robinson than the slick machines of AI. McCarey has been doing this for some time – his volume *Collected Contraptions* appeared in 2011 – but his most recent work, *The Syllabary (A Poem in 2,272 Parts)*, simultaneously published online and in book form (the book runs to eleven volumes), takes this to a new level. The result is one of the longest poems in the language, rivalling Michael Drayton's *Poly-Olbion* of 1612, which ran to 15,000 lines.

In the Foreword to the printed version (a limited edition of twenty-five, each weighing around 5kg) McCarey cryptically describes the mechanism as follows: '*The Syllabary* sets every monosyllabic word of my ideolect in a matrix of 20 initials, 10 vowels and 18 terminal consonants or nonsonants. Of the 3,600 [20 x 10 x 18] cells in the matrix, 2,272 contain a word or cluster of words. There is a glyph to every cell, and a lyric to each word-bearing glyph.' If this leaves you puzzled, the workings of McCarey's machine become luminously clear when you read the online version of the book. Here the reader enters what at first seems like an endless labyrinth – a '3D map' where there 'is no telling where it will take you' – but its fundamental mechanism quickly comes into focus. The first thing you see, turning to the bottom right-hand corner of the webpage, is a wheel, or three wheels, one inside the other, the outer wheel bearing consonants (the twenty initial consonants), the middle wheel vowels (the ten vowels), the inner wheel more consonants (the eighteen terminal consonants), and when the turning wheels come to rest they highlight a sequence of letters: HAM, LEB, HAL, YEL and so on. In the case of YEL (one of the 2,272 cells that contains a word), once the wheel stops, a handwritten glyph appears, spelling the word YELL, then we hear the poet read a poem generated by the word:

> To yell at your colleagues
> Is maybe cathartic
> But not, in the long run,
> That wise.

On other occasions the three letters in the wheel give rise to more complicated glyphs, where by the insertion of additional letters, multiple words are created, as in YEARN, which is the basis of the poem 'Yen':

> I yearn for you
> But never learn. For you
> I'd die my dear, but don't.

And then there are numerous poems which take this process as far as it can go, giving rise to complicated glyphs that by inserting extra letters create matrices of overlapping words. In the following example, the glyph

containing the words 'gunge', 'gulch', 'grudge', and 'grunge' forms the building blocks of the following poem:

> There's some gunge in the gulch
> You could guddle for bargains
> That nobody'd grudge you
> So lee aff the grunge.

The method, which you can begin to glimpse here, frequently gives rise to poems built around clusters of similar-sounding words, something which many traditional poets achieve by employing end rhyme, but here the music is created *within* the lines as well as at the end. This makes for an original and arresting soundscape, very different, in fact, from *any* use of rhyme, end rhyme or internal rhyme alike, for here the echoing sounds are constantly metamorphosing and diverging as we read. And it gives space to the reader, too, not just in allowing them to participate in the act of composition, by seeing the writing process as it unfolds, but in the latent suggestion that each poem, each word cluster, could be resolved in different ways, be rewritten by each reader. In a work containing 2,272 poems, inevitably some will be better than others. Several of the pieces here are throw-away two-liners, though even these are often infused with sardonic wit: 'In the random snooker hall of physics / Life's a glitch'. Occasionally, too, the poem strains to encompass the words thrown up by the machine, like a juggler presented with too many balls, but in the vast majority of cases, and triumphantly in others – as in the moving poem in memory of the poet Douglas Oliver – the poems rise to the occasion, at once enabled by, and transcending, the machine out of which they are born.

Bibliography

Betts, Gregory, *If Language* (Toronto: Book Thug, 2005).

Eliot, T.S., *Collected Poems* (London: Faber, 1963).

Emmerson, Stephen, *A Box of Ideas* (Malmö: Timglaset Editions, 2023).

Haffenden, John, *Poets in Conversation* (London: Faber, 1981).

Heaney, Seamus, *Seeing Things* (London: Faber, 1991).

Heidegger, Martin, *Poetry, Language, Thought*, transl. Albert Hofstadter (London: Harper & Row, 1975).

Hill, Selima, *Women in Comfortable Shoes* (Hexham: Bloodaxe, 2023).

Mallarmé, Stéphane, *Selected Poetry and Prose*, ed. Mary Ann Caws (New York: New Directions, 1982).

Martinez de las Rivas, Toby, *Floodmeadow* (London: Faber, 2023).

McCarey, Peter, *The Syllabary*: www.thesyllabary.com

Motion, Andrew, and Regan, Stephen (eds.), *The Penguin Book of Elegy* (London: Penguin, 2023).

Owen, Wilfred, *Collected Letters*, ed. Harold Owen and John Bell (London: Oxford University Press, 1967).

Pollard, Clare, *Look, Clare, Look!* (Hexham: Bloodaxe, 2005).

Reynolds, Oliver, *Seven Romes Eight* (London: Sosban, 2023).

Stillman, Frances, *The Poet's Manual and Rhyming Dictionary* (London: Thames and Hudson, 1966).

Terry, Philip, *An Attempt at Exhausting the Translation of the First Sentence of Proust's À la recherche du temps perdu* (Santiago de Chile: Crater Press, 2024).

Thwaite, Anthony (ed.), *Selected Letters of Philip Larkin* (London: Faber, 1992).

Two Poems

ANGELA LEIGHTON

Naples Metro

From here you go...
                    down through the subterranean stone
where no plants grow.
                    We're numbered, turnstiled all one way.
Don't panic. Dream.
                    TOLEDO. DANTE. The train doors close
on us, though we're
                    messaging still where the living live
so far above.
                    Then distance snaps the words we send,
and speed deletes
                    the sounds, airbrushes signs to streaks.
Now all we have's
                    in manuscript: graffiti calls
of rage, abuse,
                    maps of scrawl on darkened windows.

                              This lad leans close –
                                        tattoo'd teaser, one arm gripping
                              my chair so the figured
                                        print comes clear. What's this? stirring
                              in a movie of ink,
                                        some hoodie, pusher? I decipher only
                              a black-veiled weeper
                                        bowed to a tomb. She's moved, cartooning
                              as the train sways
                                        riffling her shape – and drops a tear,
                              or winks, maybe,
                                        crossed by the tension of a tendon stretched.
                              For grief's a scar
                                        flexed, muscled on the living thing.
                              This toughie knows
                                        how secretive the graphics of the skin.

Next stop, DANTE.
                    From here you go... The line's a tune.
This train will slow...
                    and some must leave, while others stay.
The lad's arm weeps
                    two tears of ink, and a superscripted
cross appears:
                    per Sil, *Silvia*. Who she? I think –
sister, friend?
                    funerary monument or pastoral lament?
So flesh resurrects
                    the dead in epitaph – a needle, live-streamed.
Hard not to feel
                    the point of it. (Next stop, relent:
la città dolente.)
                    Grief's a nib, life writing on skin.

Le Fontanelle

[*The body of the poet, Leopardi, was probably thrown in the mass grave at Le Fontanelle, Naples, in 1837.*]

A homely crowd
        familiars, lookalikes, stacked in piles
and all-eyes at us
        starey, agog, like crocks in a potting shed
seasonal set-asides.
        Someone has put these heads together
compiled a crowd
        of luckless souls disposed in rough ground –
tens of thousands –
        skulls set high, grinning spellbound.

        I'm touched by these
            dreamy bone heads, cuddly keepsakes,
        and reach a hand . . .
            perhaps to snatch a blessing, win
        an insight, a word.
            Are you here, Giacomo? raised high and dry
        above the cholera trench.
            Now just a candle lights the thought:
        infinite spaces
            your brain conceived, your poetry caught.

I trace these small joins –
        zips of bone still puzzled together
feathering the plates.
        (*Fontanelles.*) Long closed on themselves,
such lightning strips
        can shed no light on the secret within.
I comb the dark
        of these bone-caves, mounds of shade,
searching, searching
        death's comic act, last identity parade.

Two Free Translations and a Weather-Warning

CAROL RUMENS

Wanderer's Night-Song

(after Goethe's 'Wandrers Nachtlied')

The wind has dropped
asleep the hills
are silence-steeped
no forest rustles
wings are still.
And you? You will
yes in unslept
unrest find rest

Ice, Eden

(after Paul Celan's 'Eis, Eden')

There is a land called Lost   a moon
is flowing in its reeds
and everything once frozen
as we were frozen   sees

and warms its power of vision
from two bright earths   the night
the night the lye's corrosion
this eye-child brings to light

It sees it sees we're seeing
thou seest and I see
the time of ice   its freeing
from time   its rising free.

Dazzle

The rain at the end of the world throws itself down
Like a child breeding a tantrum
Weeping itself into a sudden thousand
Fists pausing only to freshen the mayhem
Or a last-days oil-king whirling his wheel-chair or
The drunk pissing every brain-cell
Into oblivion for the mega Now
Of a sizzling star up there
At the top of the world remade
In a blaze of music love achievable
Credible self-worth, no relation
To grief-time for the ruin, any how
No-one's listening everything's talking what the flaming hell

So the rain dazzles down for the kill

On First Looking into Dylan Thomas – III

ANDREW MCNEILLIE

That what the headlines made of Thomas was a gross travesty has long been asserted by poets and writers; some, like Louis MacNeice, who had worked with him at the BBC; others who knew him closely like Vernon Watkins; those who had done so since his boyhood like Daniel Jones; and many more. Nonetheless it still seems necessary to labour the point about the man and the mask, the writer and the bard, what Thomas called 'the colour of saying' ('The gentle seaslides of saying') and the saying. Just mention him in some circles and the first thing you'll be told, firmly, is that: 'The jury is still out'. Or that his 'durability' remains in question.[1] Or that his example was one to recover from, as from the DTs.[2] But then the 'jury' is always out. And not just on Dylan Thomas. It is in the Heraclitean nature of things. Only consider the tortuous reception, down the centuries, of (Thomas's deep love) John Donne to grasp the point, or that of Gerard Manley Hopkins, both of whom may be said, one of the sixteenth and seventeenth, the other of the nineteenth century, to have been reinvented as twentieth-century poets. Then, as individuals, we find our affections for a poet's work waxing and waning and waxing again down our lifetimes. It isn't that we exhaust them, but they exhaust us. We need time apart to re-charge our batteries, to learn once more how absence makes the heart grow fonder. How poems move on, as if behind our backs.[3]

So far Dylan Thomas has clearly not slipped through the floorboards or been consigned to oblivion on what Paul Muldoon has called 'the threshing-floor'.[4] How not? Because he also survives not only for Welsh literary history and scholarship but also, and tellingly, among what he called 'the strangers', the irrepressibly wilful, feral readers who still people the globe and know what they like. Perhaps he's even been helped along in America by the supposed (disputed and denied) homage paid him in the renaming of Robert Allen Zimmerman as Bob Dylan. But above all, Thomas lives on because for some folk the obscurity question is, somehow, part and parcel of the deal. So it was to William Empson. Should we consider these poems as an ur-kind of what has come to be called 'Language Poetry'? There is a case to be made, if not one as clear-cut a one as for W.S. Graham, who, it may be reasonably claimed, pioneered the concept. He fell under Thomas's spell early and took a long time to escape from it, becoming in his poems, eventually, something of a theoretician of language and cognition, as Thomas certainly never did.

There is much that is obscure, too, in Thomas's early, symbolic stories, more or less coeval with the early poems. These works can sometimes be bafflingly disorientating, but seek out 'The Horse's Ha', 'The Burning Baby', 'The Holy Six'[5] and beyond them those collected in *The Map of Love*, to get a taste of Thomas's macabre imagination, his eerie gothicism, his living dead, his then preoccupation with interior and exterior worlds, with childhood, youth and sexuality, with God's own patriarchy, the damned and damning hellfire clergy, with hauntings, with madness, with guilt, with incest, with murder. In some ways reading the earlier stories is like stepping into a teenager's bedroom only to find oneself through the looking-glass, lost without a map, in the curious wonderland of the Jarvis Hills where they are mostly set.

It is illuminating to trace one or two of these stories to their original places and contexts of publication. Take for example the short-lived *Contemporary Poetry and Prose* (four issues only, all in 1936), edited by the nineteen-year-old young communist, aspiring poet and novelist Roger Roughton (1916–41). He published work by Empson ('Courage Means Running'), David Gascoyne (then also aged nineteen), E.E. Cummings (sic), Gavin Ewart and George Barker. There was a clutch of celebrated surrealists, including Éluard, Breton and Dalí, also Jarry and (poems by) Picasso, as well as poems by Thomas and the stories 'The Burning Baby' and 'The School for Witches'. The contributor note on Thomas reads: 'a minor journalist and major poet, spends much of his time in Wales. He has one book of Eighteen Poems published... another collection coming out shortly.'

Such a provenance helps put things in perspective. We are in something like an undergraduate world, albeit one enjoying unusually sophisticated contacts. Whatever else, these early experiments in fiction are, in the end, with one or two exceptions, largely too amorphous structurally, too unanchored in externals, to be thor-

1 As by Seamus Heaney, in his Oxford lecture 'Dylan the Durable? On Dylan Thomas', *The Redress of Poetry* (Faber, 1995). T.S. Eliot was more certain than Heaney and believed Thomas likely to stand the test of time. See Robert Crawford, *Eliot After The Waste Land* (2022), p. 225. He would have published him, but missed out, as he missed out with *Ulysses* to Bodley Head.

2 Michael Longley, in 'Patrick Kavanagh': 'I was then recovering from a late-adolescent Dylan binge, unable to see the word for the D.T.s...' *Sidelines: Selected Prose 1916–2015* (Enitharmon Press, 2017).

3 Michael Longley's responses to Dylan Thomas are a case in point, as he makes clear in an interview: 'The Time of the Singing of Birds has Come', in the magazine *The Dark Horse*, Winter 2022–23. The bout of *delirium tremens* was temporary and understandable. His appreciation of and admiration for the poet steadied and recovered itself through time but only admitted the late poems.

4 Paul Muldoon, 'To the Threshing-Floor', *TLS,* 18 January 2002.

5 'The Horse's Ha', *Janus*, May 1936. 'The Burning Baby', *Contemporary Poetry and Prose*, No. 1, May 1936. 'The Holy Six', *Contemporary Poetry & Prose*, No. 9, Spring 1937.

oughly rewarding. Surely Vernon Watkins was right when he prevailed on Thomas to take the turn towards the realism we find in the stories in *A Portrait of the Artist as a Young Dog*. Watkins, his devoted friend and champion, regularly provided invaluable advice, as Thomas showed him his latest poems and other productions in progress. The *Young Dog* stories gave free rein to Thomas's comic gifts, his eye for character, ear for speech, his sheer *nous* and quick psychological insight. They show him to be a tough narrator, ready to disappoint sentimental expectation, or hope of a 'happy' ending. Here, and in his broadcast reminiscences, we find him, too, a marvellous celebrant of the sea in all its humours, and of the seaside; of Swansea itself, and, not least, its nightlife, its Orwellian down-and-outness and ruin; of holidays and outings; of snow and, of course, of childhood and the child's eye view.

*

In a gathering of tributes on the death of the poet published in *Encounter*, in January 1954, Louis MacNeice went to the heart of things. 'When his first work appeared it was astonishingly new and yet went back to the oldest of our roots – roots which had long been ignored, written off, or simply forgotten. He was not just a poet among poets; he was, as has often been remarked, a bard, with the three great bardic virtues of faith, joy, and craftsmanship – and, one could add, of charity... Many of his poems are obscure but it is never the obscurity of carelessness; though I, for one, assumed it might be when I first read his early work in the 1930s.' MacNeice did much to set the record straight, as he saw the matter, and from his knowledge of Thomas as a highly professional colleague at the BBC. (See some of the more journalistic broadcasts.) MacNeice paid further homage to 'this strange kind of poet' in the character of 'Gwilym', in his long poem *Autumn Sequel* (1954 – Canto XVIII 'Lament for the Makers').

Beyond the obscurity question, there is another charge regularly brought against Thomas: one concerning maturity. The line taken is that Thomas 'never grew up' either as man or poet, if the two can be separated. On the contrary, he regressed. His poetry began in adolescence and ended in childhood. It is a weak joke. But the implication is that such a thing is clearly not good enough in grown-up company. So the prosecution rest their case, spicing it, too, as they do so, with humourless accusations of sentimentality, levelled especially at *Under Milk Wood*.

You must and will reach your own verdict. But bear in mind that Thomas, in the footballing metaphor, always played the poem, not the poet. It was the poem he cared about, not its author, or the canon. Great poems make great poets, not the other way about, as the Czech poet Vladimír Holan once put it. Thomas gave many public readings of other poets' work on this basis. It is perhaps the only honest route to take. Give their proper due to brilliant poems like 'I see the boys of summer', 'The force that through the green fuse drives the flower', 'Our Eunuch Dreams', 'Especially when the October wind', 'The hand that signed the paper', 'Should Lanterns Shine', 'And death shall have no dominion', 'Altarwise by owl-light', 'After the Funeral', 'Once it was the colour of saying', 'The Hunchback in the Park' and so on. I have already omitted too many to get that far and that is nowhere near the end. My list is very long, and that is just for the poems. There is another for the prose.

Reviews

Revolting into Style

Michael Nott, *Thom Gunn: A Cool Queer Life* (Faber) £25

Reviewed by N.S. Thompson

To write a poem about Elvis Presley in 1956 – even a serious one – was quite extraordinary, especially if you were a twenty-seven-year-old Cambridge graduate on the road to becoming an English professor. Perhaps not so surprising if you were living in the United States and attracted to handsome young men in leather. But, at that time, same sex attraction was a taboo subject, same sexual relations between men were illegal, and among poetry circles the subject matter of the new rock-and-roll music would have been deemed frivolous, if considered at all. But this was Thom Gunn. One only had to look at the way he spelled his name, changed legally from Thomas to Thomson to honour his mother, Charlotte Thomson, who took her own life when Gunn was fifteen. Tragically for her two sons, Thom and Ander (Alexander), they were the ones to discover her body lying on the sitting room floor in her dressing gown, a gas poker stuck into her mouth.

Although devastated, Gunn remained outwardly cool. He reserved hatred for his father, a successful newspaper editor, who had been divorced from his mother five years before. After her death, Gunn was able to continue his education courtesy of family friends in Hampstead, spending vacations with his mother's many sisters in rural Kent. Being an able scholar at private school, if not particularly good at Latin, he was accepted to read English at Trinity College, Cambridge, in October 1950, after serving his two years obligatory National Service in the army as an educational sergeant.

It was at Cambridge that the rather timid schoolboy blossomed into a poet. He had begun writing poetry as a teenager, reading his Dylan Thomas and Auden (the New Apocalyptics having waned) but was more influenced by the Renaissance and Jacobean poetry he read, as well as the Romantics, especially Keats. He followed these poets in formal or informal rhyme and metre and was able to make a name for himself by publishing (and editing) the undergraduate magazines of the day. And in those days, London editors were on the *qui vive* for who might emerge from Oxbridge, such was the cache and prestige it enjoyed. Thus by the time he graduated, Gunn had published a collection, *Fighting Terms* (Fantasy Press, 1954) and made influential connections that would lead to his inclusion in Robert Conquest's *New Lines* anthology (1956) and, later, his first collection with Faber, *The Sense of Movement* (1957).

In the meantime, he had met and fallen in love with a young visiting American student, Mike Kitay and, so as to be with him, had applied, successfully, for postgraduate work in America. Thus in August 1954, Gunn set sail on the Queen Elizabeth to New York, and continued by train to California to start postgraduate work with the renowned poet and critic Yvor Winters at Berkeley. This may raise eyebrows, given Gunn's later life, but the crusty old didact took a shine to the keen and garrulous young Englishman and they remained on very friendly relations for the rest of Winters's life. However able he was, Gunn never progressed to a further degree, preferring to teach, which he did – off and on – for the rest of his life.

The rest of the story becomes more familiar. Thom and Mike were able to settle in San Francisco and were there for the great Sixties cultural boom, enjoying the hippie life of be-ins and love-ins, Grateful Dead concerts in Golden Gate Park, accompanied by any number of chemical stimulants, often courtesy of entrepreneurial manufacturers such as Owsley Stanley. But with the Eighties, of course, came the terrible scourge of AIDS and the end of the bathhouse culture so ably portrayed in Armistead Maupin's novels. It was not, however, the end of Gunn's promiscuous life. While the bond remained with Mike Kitay, the relationship had ceased to be a sexual one and while Kitay was 'serially monogamous', this was not the case with his housemate, who was addicted to habitual cruising as well as formidable drug taking. Nevertheless, they eventually bought a large duplex in Haight-Ashbery and were keen to establish a 'family' there with other invited residents.

Gunn's was thus a highly sensual life right up to the end. Indeed, it was the end of his life. In April 2004, Kitay and other residents discovered his body in his room after no one had seen him for a day, but heard the television and comings and goings during the night. The coroner pronounced 'acute polysubstance abuse' as the cause of death.

As to the poetry, Nott is deft at showing how Gunn was able to aggrandize young motorcyclists into existential heroes, most famously in his early 'One the Move' where

> their hum
> Bulges to thunder held by calf and thigh...
>
> ... and at best,
> Reaching no absolute, in which to rest,
> One is always nearer by not keeping still.

These 'self-defined, astride the created will' are tempered by the elevated impersonal pronoun 'one' which Gunn came to regret. However, his phrase 'revolt into a style' in the 'Elvis Presley' poem became an iconic phrase for the whole 'rebel without a cause' generation and was adopted by George Melly for the title of his 1970 book on pop culture. But Gunn was far from a 'pop' poet. Where many poets, especially in America, had turned from metre to free verse, Gunn was more measured. In fact, he found it difficult to lose the music of pentameters from his head and only managed it via writing first in syllabics and from there moving to free verse. This despite being a fan of another iconoclast in Robert Duncan, who had been openly gay from the 1940s, and writing on him. But that same freedom escaped Gunn. In the sequence 'The Geysers' (1972) the broken lines look like late Carlos Williams, but are actually rhyming pentameter couplets:

> torn from the self
>   in which I breathed and trod
> I am
>   I am raw meat
>   I am a god

It is the ecstatic side of Thom Gunn that Michael Nott emphasises. Drawing heavily on Gunn's letters (which he edited in 2021), his book also benefits from a rich sheaf of photographs.

Dark Vibrant Spaces

Selina Nwulu, *A Little Resurrection* (Bloomsbury) £7.99; Solmaz Sharif, *Customs* (Bloomsbury) £8.99

Reviewed by Kayleigh Jayshree

Bloomsbury's recent publications tend to engage traumatic histories, diasporic stories and motherhood while being formally inventive. Selina Nwulu's *A Little Resurrection* has titles, themes and images that repeat, adding texture and character to a typical poem, for example in 'Cords That Cannot Be Broken':

> travelling continents, clinging to the cross
> for protection and our tongues an heirloom
>
> carrying the continuum of time;
> Sunday School ritual, greased hair

The images refer to chosen family and actual family, but the title is more conventional than the language in the poem. When Nwulu writes more difficult, oblique poems, like 'Fisherman At Ouakam Beach, Dakar', they connect more surely:

> I am in awe of how much the landscape
> wants them, extends its hospitality through the
>   sun,
> its rays an opening blossom seeking only
> to fortify their blackness, the two-tier blue
> of sky and sea illuminating the contours
> of their silhouettes.

Throughout, Nwulu is painterly in her use of colour, belonging and movement. Awe in these poems coexists with scientific language, natural images, shadow, beauty, darkness and light.

Solmaz Sharif's *Customs* invokes deliberate distance and separation, but without recourse to formal language to draw in her readers. Sharif uses an extended metaphor of the airport customs, referencing this liminal space closely in the poems 'Visa' and 'Social Skills Training', whose questions include:

> *What the fuck are you crying for, officer?* the
> wire mother teaches me to say, while studies
>   suggest *Solmaz,*
> *have you thanked your executioner today?*

Like recent collections by Joe Carrick-Varty and Victoria Chang, *Customs* concludes with a long poem, 'An Otherwise', which plays with space, texture and form, to speak to previous poems in the collection and relay a tonal shift in their work. 'An Otherwise' ends:

> I set out, as she set out
> armed, later than I would
> like, to follow

the music mine

and not, but matrilineal
and in the amniotic sac

of sound
reaching where the listening

ends and the mind alights
in that dim red glow

I wipe clean my blade
I tap at the door

I pass through there so that

Sharif's intention is clear in the way the lines are structured: the careful line breaks and sparing punctuation add to the dark vibrant space 'An Otherwise' inhabits. Ending a collection that explores so many themes with a birthing scene, and mid-sentence, could seem contrived; instead it serves to draw together Sharif's themes.

The long poem is more convincing than Sharif's extended metaphor of airport customs as limbo. As with Nwulu's, Sharif's poems' parental bonds connect us fiercely with the theme of the proximity of life and death.

Borrowed Light

Peter Vertacnik, *The Nature of Things Fragile: Poems* (Criterion Books) £17.99

Reviewed by Kevin Gardner

If you use the social media platform X, you will likely know Peter Vertacnik from his thoughtfully curated Forgotten Good Poems, a beacon of civilisation in the three-ring circus that Elon Musk's Twitter has become. Vertacnik is now the winner of the New Criterion Prize, given to a 'manuscript of poems that pay close attention to form'. If you are keen on formalist poetry – and really, who wouldn't be? – then you will be entranced by *The Nature of Things Fragile*, Vertacnik's debut collection, which showcases many traditional poetic forms (sonnet, sestina, villanelle, epigram, double triolet, and so on) as well as a wide variety of newly invented forms. Though he is an adroit formalist, Vertacnik also writes poems of freer structures and rhymeless patterns, giving a satisfying variety to the book while masking some of the intentionality of craft. Nevertheless, the collection's formalism is its prevailing effect, and the delicate beauty and intricate structures of the poems invite comparisons to Richard Wilbur and Anthony Thwaite.

As one might gather from his title, Vertacnik immerses the reader in the fragility of living things, and not unexpectedly the collection is dominated by elegiac tones. Some poems are threnodies on the deaths or declining illnesses of loved ones, while others are laments on a past that cannot be recovered, often in subtle but sure-footed iambics: an old photo of his parents, with wrinkles airbrushed, 'designed to free / this likeness from time's price'; candles, guttering, 'reminding us how shadows shift'; the poet's mirrored reflection, 'holding fast to its brief and borrowed light'. In 'Art', the speaker exposes a childhood sorrow to which he has become inured, yet shocks the reader with the devastating revelation. It's an extraordinary opening to the collection, not least because the poem ends with the admission, 'I lied'. It's the very nature of art to deceive even as it reveals, but we are also reminded that deception is inherent in some of our most honest expressions. I think this is what Vertacnik alludes to in 'Gray Areas': 'Implication and allusion divert / our words like bends / in a stream'.

Other fragilities are interwoven: former homes and towns reduced to the rubble of memory, commonplace objects and experiences now absent in our digital lives. These too strike an elegiac note: the 'departed blur' of home movies; the 'barren baritone' of a landline's dial tone; 'the hiss from analog / recordings'. 'In Praise of Blank Cassettes' entwines a joyful memory of outmoded recording technology with a wistful memory of making and gifting mixtapes:

it was in the compilation of brief tracks
(tunes which enticed, then pleaded) that
  I excelled,
those missives made of ballads snatched from
  the airwaves –
just as swallows were ensnared in nets for
  counting,
but released again into an evening breeze
where they soon warbled... so my ardent tapes
alighted shyly on the waiting palms

of former loves. One is grateful for these warbling interludes of playfulness – including the substantial central section of witty epigrams – that counterbalance his poems of remembered sorrow.

Not that the collection is gloomy or oppressive; even the most funereal poem, 'The Fenced Field', which imagines the inevitability of decomposition that follows burial ('A dark mound lists and settles' above 'the earth's digesting undertow'), is answered by 'Constitutional', a poem of regeneration: though 'The morning sky / resembles our faded / tablecloth, azure once, / its linen long / paled with age', the speaker is nonetheless 'alive beneath that / slowly renewing blue'. If not quite hope itself, then hopefulness: *The Nature of Things Fragile* embodies a habit of hope, sculpted like a marble effigy in the beauty and order of its lines and forms. In this way, Vertacnik, like Larkin, aims 'to prove / Our almost-instinct almost true'.

What Else Will You Love Me Despite?

Armen Davoudian, *The Palace of Forty Pillars* (Corsair) £10.99

Reviewed by Alex Mepham

Armen Davoudian's debut collection *The Palace of Forty Pillars* spans time, geography and culture. The child falls asleep while reading *The Book of Kings*, secretly glinting fingers adorned with fish scales against the light. The adult enters their own, teaching poetry at an elite university. Crawling through poison ivy, falling in love at 'German Camp', the origin story of a parent's marriage in 1989 Isfahan. This collection examines a complex identity, and explores what holds the subject to and grounds it in these identities. Most powerfully, the life of the senses defines the poems: mother's cooking, juice of blackberries and pomegranates, and particularly fragrances: sharing rosewater shampoo with mother, men who smell of fenugreek, the intimacy of saffron.

These poems are tender, intricately negotiating a queer identity within a family's love and expectation, balancing its abrasions against the socially conservative Islamic Republic of Iran, and observing how easily this balancing act is fumbled.

The book's sonnet, ghazal and rubaiyat forms, and recourse to rhyme, anchor the poems in song. The blurb describes this collection as 'formally radical', though one could argue calling upon these centuries-old forms can be seen as the antithesis of radical. At times the poems are less agile in phrasing, with some awkward formal results, e.g., 'The West is stealing clouds from Persian skies / Death to America! Militarize!' ('The Ring'); 'where they used to have ammo. / A mother shouts, *te amo*' ('Passage').

Debuts can risk overdoing formal display. Some features appear merely performative, as in the crown-of-sonnets sequence 'The Ring': one sonnet section, instead of a rhyme scheme, uses phonetic palindromes, which is interesting, but the capitalisation of these palindromic elements felt overemphatic.

Whereas the 'Ring' sequence falls short, the title sequence of twenty sonnets 'The Palace of Forty Pillars' succeeds, documenting the different generations' characters and domestic life. Engaging and full of tenderness, this sequence maps the speaker's place and role within the family as the son, and contrasts it with the roles of other family members: mother prepares a spread of home-cooked food, father stews tea and tucks the son in bed, grandma preserves crushed garlic. The son plays the expected role (drawing a naked girl on a paper plane) but recognises the pleasure in transgression, writing a test cheat-sheet in Armenian on a friend's chest.

The most successful poems here rhyme nimbly, without technique being the focal exploit. Davoudian is capable of elegance, notably in the opening poem 'Coming Out of the Shower', where rhymes morph into half-rhymes as we walk through the lines and conclude on the killer-question: 'What else will you love me despite?' Likewise, the devastating ghazal 'Swan Song', the title poem from Davoudian's debut pamphlet, and the final poem of this collection, 'Saffron', show Davoudian's ability to work with feather-light fragility.

Alive-alive-oh

Kerry Hardie, *We Go On* (Bloodaxe) £12

Reviewed by Lenni Sanders

The style of Kerry Hardie's ninth collection, *We Go On*, is elegant, plain-spoken, matter of fact and precise. Like Gillian Clarke's, her poems respond to the natural world. As in her earlier work, poems often come in short lines like 'Gaunt trees, stark against the sky. / Running water, stilled' ('Back Where We Began'). Lines can be sentence fragments like these, or be split up by commas into breaths, as part of a run-on sentence of a stanza.

In 'Witness', about standing in the garden on a spring evening as night falls, the speaker says, without lamenting, 'Ah world, you don't know, / you don't care, / whether I love you or not'. The indifferent seasons are a recurring theme throughout the collection, with the passing of time being paid careful attention. Seasons imply change as well as loss, as in the poem of mourning 'The Departure': 'He went. The branches tangled together. / The world closed quietly over.'

While *We Go On* is often concerned with death, it feels very much alive. This duality is clear in 'The Muse is a Red Dog' in which the dog, 'giddy with joy, / frolics about on the graves / because he is still alive-alive-oh / and May is as green as the grass / and the dead are there, all around him, / scampering about in the light'. Hardie is conscious that the poems' observational strengths might lead readers to overlook her metaphysical interests. Hardie's red dog, she writes in the notes, is 'a personal symbol of the creative unconscious' – this longer poem stands out in the collection, an image Hardie has used before, coming to full maturity.

If 2014's *The Zebra Stood in the Night* suffered at times from a similar anxiety about time, with its references to screens and apps, there is little of that sort to date *We Go On*. Most of the new poems feel timeless. A presence, directly named as 'God' in 'September Light', fills these poems. Elsewhere, there is a sense of pantheism. The sky (which like 'the air' recurs throughout) appears in 'Whose Is the Song?' as a 'witness'. In 'Search' there is a 'secret running under life'.

The poems of *We Go On* which *are* clearly rooted in a specific period usually specify the year in which the events described occur. Although the speaker is often describing a memory, the year is being considered as a cultural and geopolitical moment, or large-scale tragedy, as much as a personal history. 'Just Another Bomb, Belfast 1974' is a poem about the Troubles; 'Empires' is set in 2003, days before the US invaded Iraq. 'News from Ireland 1348' addresses the plague.

But it is not the historical poems which most endure in memory. In 'Pain', the speaker looks at a faded print showing an old man tending to pigs on a hill. The turn in the final stanza is astonishing – 'Yet his pigs rootle, blacker and busier / they grub through the flesh of my shoulder, / their hooves dig, cloven and sharp.' The pain could be physical or could be grief – it feels to me that the way in which the pigs escape the print to wound the speaker is similar to how they then escape the poem to wound the reader.

Thrust Outward

André Naffis-Sahely, *High Desert* (Bloodaxe) £10.99; Luke Samuel Yates, *Dynamo* (Smith|Doorstop) £10.99; Sarah Fletcher, *Plus Ultra* (Cheerio) £11

Reviewed by Bebe Ashley

André Naffis-Sahely's *High Desert* journeys from the American Southwest to Mexico, Switzerland, Bangladesh and Crete. This work quickly focuses our attention on the uncomfortable inevitably of artificial borders: 'Consider the border, / any border. If a border is a war zone, then what do the insides of our consciousness look like?' ('Ode to the Errant King') and the personal connections to people on other sides: 'in my head, an email from my mother / that read, "we're doomed, save what you can"' ('The Other Side of Nowhere').

The horrors of history are sometimes eased into the poems: in 'Maybe the People Don't Want to Live and Let Live', he begins 'Sun-drunk, I roll / along the streets of Los Angeles, / while the radio rewrites / the world as I know it' and historic intervention appears across all five parts of the collection: 'Driving in every direction / down licks of red road, / I have lost myself in militarized topography' ('Roadrunners').

The penultimate section of 'A People's History of the West' works well in its use of 'found poems', as Naffis-Sahely describes them. He manipulates the written and spoken language of historical figures, including Muriel Rukeyser and her FBI file: 'other poems by this author could not / have been written except in a period / of disordered economics'. Perhaps it is also true of Naffis-Sahely that the poems of *High Desert* couldn't have been written except in this period of global disorder.

High Desert uses historical reflections and asks readers to consider their evolving role in an unpredictable future on an increasingly hostile Earth: 'How many / rocks and stars shall we visit / until we remember we're human?' ('Ode to the Errant King'). At times it leans further into its 'psychedelic journal', nature, a phrase which seems also to fit Luke Samuel Yates's *Dynamo* and Sarah Fletcher's *Plus Ultra*.

Dynamo won the Poetry Business 2022 International Book & Pamphlet Competition. It builds on Yates's previous 2014/15 Poetry Business Pamphlet Competition win, *The Flemish Primitives,* from which some poems re-emerge. A dynamo is a machine in which you are responsible for producing your own propulsion through a journey: this is a fitting title for a collection that begins with the aspiration of 'Going Somewhere' and ends with the reliability of 'Drying, folding, putting away' ('The Laundry').

In the first section, the propulsion feels as though it might leap out of control at any moment. A frantic energy is created by repetition and natural speech patterns, as in 'The Bikers': 'The bikers climb the path we're coming down, / here they come now, from the beach / where there might be seals, should we / ask them if they've seen any seals? / We're asking them if they've seen the seals.' In 'The Frisbee', 'The frisbee flies / like a moon orbiting the weekend' while in 'Desert Boots' greater emotional risks are taken in the poems: 'Last summer it seemed / nothing would ever change / but today you are a person / who wears desert boots / and might fall in love'.

The simple numbering of the sections doesn't give much away about the grouping or ordering of poems. A shift of style or focus is recognisable between section breaks. A mid-poem statement in 'The Mystery Shopper' might also highlight Yates's greater preoccupation in these poems: 'All this is banter. / But mainly you are just a conveyor belt / for thinking about / endings'. It is in his endings that sentimentality and loneliness creep into *Dynamo* where 'All kinds of possibilities / are slipping away' ('Can't'); where 'I move away so slow / you don't know / I'm going' ('Moving'); where 'The lights change on an empty crossing' ('Hotpot').

Sentimentality rarely lingers in Sarah Fletcher's *Plus Ultra:* although she shares Yates's fondness for a casual tone in poem titles. Fletcher's voices powerfully embrace honest conversation with each other: 'you fucking dirty pigeon of a man' ('Capitulation').

Plus Ultra is the first poetic offering from Cheerio, with Cheerio poetry editor Martha Sprackland building its inaugural list. Fletcher has published pamphlets consistently since 2015. Previous works include *Kissing Angels* (Dead Ink), *Typhoid August* (Poetry Business) and *Caviar* (Out-Spoken), but *Plus Ultra* marks her debut in a collection that extends 'further beyond' the knowable and concrete existence of the tangible world. It takes its title from the Pillars of Hercules near the Straits of Gibraltar (*Ne plus ultra*/Nothing further beyond) and, throughout, fully exploits the exclamation mark as an underused poetic tool.

The inclusion of a translation and 'a version' (as Fletcher puts it) of the nineteenth-century Spanish poet Enrique Gil y Carrasco's 'The Violet' emphasises Fletcher's enjoyment of discovery and reimagining. 'Here I am: a bouquet of past voices', Fletcher's translation opens, apt for a work that references Frank O'Hara, Rainer Maria Rilke and Ezra Pound alongside song lyrics from the Eagles or a performance from Sean Shibe. This is followed by Fletcher's 'version' of 'The Violet', which grounds the romantic lavishing with 'Listen! A violinist is smearing sound / across the awnings / like a glob of yellow paint', bringing her voice very much into the contemporary sphere.

The formally various *Plus Ultra* is restless: there is much for the reader to uncover in its fluency across modes. Fletcher's awareness of the writer–reader relationship keeps the work approachable: 'The poet to the reader: you don't know me! / The reader to the poem, painstakingly, repeats: You do not know me!' ('The Bed is Not a Window, the Bed is a Two-Way Mirror').

The Life We've Spilled

Richard Sanger, *Way to Go* (Biblioasis) CDN $19.95

Reviewed by Evan Jones

When the Canadian poet and playwright Richard Sanger died of pancreatic cancer on 12 September 2022, aged sixty-two, he had completed work on his fourth collection. The cancer had been diagnosed and treated in the two years preceding his death and the poems in *Way to Go* consider the uncertainty of illness and inevitability. That they do so with joy and lightness is a sign of the book's quality. 'Flâneur' tours the independent bars and restaurants of downtown Toronto and closes, 'I drank in all of you – I drink you all in, / your suds, your solace; I haven't had enough'. The unfairness of it all doesn't register – this is not a poetry of complaint but one of praise – and Sanger bustles through the poems, eyeing the streets around him.

A student of European languages, Sanger shows his cosmopolitan sympathies throughout the collection, offering a wistful translation of Baudelaire's '*Recueillement*' and a chatty response to the Brazilian poet and composer Antonio Cicero's '*Palavras aladas*'. But his poems depend on the immediate world – slices of life in Toronto embedded in community, family, love, relationships. The book opens with 'Into the Park', the speaker on his bike, riding into surroundings he knows but is equally surprised by: the 'entanglements' and 'dangers' of everyday life around him. In 'Valentine', what begins with an observation about 'our punk Juliet from down the street' hanging her washing becomes a reminiscence. The poet reimagines his own youthful love and long-term affection, '... the sheets of our bed / creased and rumpled, and the life we've spilled'.

Amid the muddiness of this kind of sentiment, Sanger shows his journalist's eye for detail, language and story, elevated by his gift for metaphor. A poem about the drowned magazine editor Blair Fraser (1909–1968), an early critic of Liberal Prime Minister Pierre Trudeau, tells a deeper truth about a life cut short. In a longish ode, the Ontario Tory politician Claude Bennett (1936–2020) becomes a figure of misspent adulthood, a criticism of the conservative turns many take in later life, where the former politician is mocked for 'the pay-offs you got, / the slush funds, the trust funds, the husbands, / the kisses, the condoms':

> ... What happened, Claude, what happened?
> For all any of us cared,
> you might as well have been a mannequin
> modelling spotless high-rise underwear
> in the Eaton's catalogue...

How does one get from the rule-breaking teen to the rule-creating adult? the poems ask. And what happens when that rule-creator's world changes? Bennett worked in provincial politics for fifteen years. His political career ended in 1987, when he was fifty-one. What then? Sure, he held jobs and positions even as he disappeared from the public eye. But what does this say about legacy? And what does a poet near the end of his life make of all this? The poem isn't an answer but makes clear that a response from someone like Bennett wouldn't help anyway.

'Canoe', a title that seems to wade in the clichéd waters of Canada, turns into a poem about something else entirely. Sanger would have known that the word was imported into English from French, where it is masculine – '*le canoë*' – but the Spanish roots, '*la canoa*', are feminine. That the word is Arawakan in origin holds the poem together. Sanger's canoe is sexualized initially, so that 'From above, her hips could bear whole families, / and their baggage into new worlds'. But then in a second section the speaker seems to change his mind, reflecting instead on how inappropriate a symbol this is:

> the canoe as the chalice
> of all the delusions we most cherish,
> the shape we took from those
> whose lands we stole to settle and hold in sway,
> and which you, the most disreputable,
> in the slimiest way imaginable,
> now liken to a woman's curves...

The reconsideration reveals a poet attached to and understanding of his world, even on his way out. Yet the consideration doesn't end there, and Sanger admits the attraction of the first metaphor, ending, 'What other vessel could you love like this?' It is not a poem about change so much as acknowledging the complexity of connections in the language and the variety of traditions that exist, problematic but part of us.

Way to Go is not groundbreaking. And though the poem 'Exit Interview' might hint at a few regrets ('Have you done what you came here to do? / Have you gone where you wanted to go?), that's not what the book is. This is the work of a poet focusing on what he loves – conversations, jokes and asides – the world around him welcomed. It is personal, emotive but never maudlin, telling of a life well lived, and the sweetness of being alive.

Some Contributors

Adrian May is an unrepentant old folkie; author of *Tradition in Creative Writing* (Palgrave), *Boot Sale Harvest* (non-fiction, Dunlin Press) and *Full Fathom Folk* (songs and poems, Rosewood Press).

Alex Wong has published two collections of verse with Carcanet: *Poems Without Irony* (2017) and *Shadow and Refrain* (2021). He is currently preparing a selection from Alice Meynell for Carcanet Classics.

Alice Entwistle is the author of several critical books and many shorter works reflecting her specialist research interest in contemporary poetry, cultural geography and literary aesthetics, particularly poetry and experimental writing by women in the UK. Until recently, she was Professor of Contemporary Literature and Textual Aesthetics at the University of South Wales.

Angela Leighton's sixth volume of poetry, 'Something, I Forget', was published in 2023 by Carcanet.

Carol Rumens lives in North Wales and writes full-time. Her most recent poetry publications are *The Mixed Urn* (Sheep Meadow, 2019) and *Bezdelki: Small Things* (The Emma Press, 2018). The latter received the Michael Marks Award for Best Pamphlet.

Poet and translator **Daniel Lipara** (Argentina) is the author of *Otra vida* (Bajolaluna), translated into English as *Another Life* by Robin Myers (Eulalia Books), and *Como la noche adentro de los ojos* (Bajolaluna).

Ian Thomson is a writer and journalist. He is the recipient of the Royal Society of Literature's Ondaatje Prize and the W.H. Heinemann Award. He is currently completing a book for Faber on the Baltic during the Second World War.

Jane Houston is a writer from Wales who has published in several UK magazines.

Judith Woolf is an Italianist who combines Holocaust-related research and translation with writing poetry and fiction. Her latest novel, *The Case of the Campus Cat*, is on sale in aid of Doctors Without Borders.

Kayleigh Jayshree is a poet and critic. Her poems have been published with *fourteen poems* and *Butcher's Dog*. Kayleigh is a member of MMU Poetry Library's Critics Collective.

Lenni Sanders is a writer living in Manchester, who has previously reviewed poetry for the *Times Literary Supplement*. Lenni's first poetry pamphlet, *Poacher*, was published by The Emma Press in 2019.

Margitt Lehbert translates poetry from and into German, e.g. work by Les Murray, Elizabeth Bishop, Carol Ann Duffy, Georg Trakl and Sarah Kirsch. In 2006 she founded the German press Edition Rugerup.

N.S. Thompson is a poet, critic and translator. He has worked as a gardener and museum curator in Italy and an academic and creative writing tutor in Oxford. His latest pamphlets are *After War* (New Walk) and *Ghost Hands* (Melos Press).

Philip Terry is a poet and experimental translator. His version of Dante's *Purgatorio*, relocating Dante to Mersea island in Essex, is forthcoming from Carcanet in October 2024.

Rebecca Watts's third poetry collection, *The Face in the Well*, will be published by Carcanet in January 2025.

Robin Myers is a US-born, Mexico-based poet and translator. Recent translations include *The Brush* by Eliana Hernández-Pachón (Archipelago Books) and *A Strange Adventure* by Eva Forest (Sternberg Press).

Roop Majumdar was born in Kolkata, India. His work has appeared in *Poetry Review*, *The Manchester Review*, *Poetry Ireland Review*, *The Bombay Literary Magazine* and *Transect Magazine*.

WWWW.PNREVIEW.CO.UK

Editors
Michael Schmidt
John McAuliffe

Editorial Manager
Andrew Latimer

Contributing Editors
Anthony Vahni Capildeo
Sasha Dugdale
Will Harris

Copyeditor
Maren Meinhardt

Designed by
Andrew Latimer

Editorial address
The Editors at the address on the right. Manuscripts cannot be returned unless accomp anied by a stamped addressed envelope or international reply coupon.

Trade distributors
Combined Book Services Ltd

Represented by
Compass IPS Ltd

Copyright
© 2024 Poetry Nation Review
All rights reserved
ISBN 978 1 80017 421 4
ISBN 0144-7076

Subscriptions—6 issues
  INDIVIDUAL–print and digital:
  £45; abroad £65
  INSTITUTIONS–print only:
  £140; abroad £162
  INSTITUTIONS–digital only:
  from Exact Editions (https://shop.exacteditions.com/gb/pn-review)
to: PN Review, Alliance House,
30 Cross Street, Manchester,
M2 7AQ, UK

Subscriptions & Enquiries:
support@pnreview.co.uk

Supported by